AMAZIN' AGAIN

AMAZIN' AGAIN

How the 2015 New York Mets
Brought the Magic Back to Queens

By Greg W. Prince

Foreword by Howie Rose

SPORTS
PUBLISHING

Sports Publishing books may be purchased in bulk at special discounts for sales promotion, corporate gifts, fund-raising, or educational purposes. Special editions can also be created to specifications. For details, contact the Special Sales Department, Sports Publishing, 307 West 36th Street, 11th Floor, New York, NY 10018 or sportspubbooks@skyhorsepublishing.com.

Sports Publishing® is a registered trademark of Skyhorse Publishing, Inc.®, a Delaware corporation.

Visit our website at www.sportspubbooks.com.

10 9 8 7 6 5 4 3 2 1

Library of Congress Cataloging-in-Publication Data is available on file.

Cover design by Tom Lau
Cover photos courtesy of AP Images
All photos in insert courtesy of AP Images

ISBN: 978-1-61321-945-4
Ebook ISBN: 978-1-61321-946-1

Printed in the United States of America

For Stephanie, Suzan, and Charles.
The Princes are a pretty good team, too.

CONTENTS

FOREWORD

I've always appreciated the talents of baseball beat writers. They work on strict deadlines, and have to present a coherent, well written, comprehensive account of a ballgame, including quotes from the participants within a short time after the game's conclusion. We're talking minutes here, not hours or days. Their product is generally outstanding.

As I write the foreword to this book, we are nearly two months removed from the conclusion of the New York Mets' 2015 National League Championship season and I'm still not sure how to even begin to explain what happened, never mind do it in a coherent, well written and comprehensive fashion.

Thankfully, that's not my job. That's where Greg Prince comes in. He's the trained professional here. He might not work on deadline, but his blog, *Faith and Fear in Flushing*, co-written with Jason Fry, is simply the most intelligent, well written and thought-provoking of its kind; clearly written by adults for adults. He's the perfect person to recount the events of one of the most memorable of the Mets' fifty-four National League seasons, in a manner that will no doubt leave you trying to figure out how they crammed so many twists and turns into just one year.

Several times during the stretch drive I remarked on the air how it felt as though the Mets had experienced three or four different seasons within the six months allocated for just one. The Jerry Blevins era seemed a lifetime ago by the time the Mets nailed down the Eastern Division title on that memorable afternoon in Cincinnati. Along the way, events started to feel eerily similar to me to other epochal moments from championship seasons past.

When the Phillies' Jeff Francoeur hit that line drive off the leg of Carlos Torres who hacky-sacked the ball to Daniel Murphy, who somehow made a perfect flip to Torres covering first for the out, were you not somehow reminded of the Pirates' Dave Augustine's "ball off the wall" in 1973? If you go back that far, and you felt at the time that plays like that are not wasted on second place finishes, wasn't that the tipoff that the division was the Mets' to be won, just as it was forty-two improbable years earlier?

Truthfully, though, a lot of what transpired during the 2015 season reminded me more of 1969 than it did any other year. The Washington Nationals (formerly the Montreal Expos, who were born and played their first game against the Mets in '69) were the Mets' opening day opponents. Sure, Max Scherzer had them no-hit into the sixth inning, but of course, the Mets found a way to win, largely thanks to a couple of Ian Desmond errors. One game, one omen. Nearly six months later, in the penultimate game of the regular season, Scherzer actually did no-hit the Mets. Just as a fellow named Bob Moose of the Pittsburgh Pirates had done to them on September 20, 1969, four days before the Mets clinched the division crown.

Five days before that, on September 15, 1969, the Cardinals' Steve Carlton dominated the Mets en route to setting a then-major league record with 19 strikeouts. Of course, Ron Swoboda hit a pair of two run homers and the Mets won, 4–3. In early September 2015, with the Mets attempting to sweep the Nationals in a three game series for the second time in a little over a month and grab firm control of the division, Washington's Stephen Strasburg was similarly dominating the Mets, who trailed late by a run. No sooner did I reflect on the air about 1969 and say that the way things were going, I half expected Ron Swoboda to pop out of the dugout and take Strasburg deep, Kelly Johnson went full-out Swoboda and hit the next pitch out for a game-tying pinch-hit homer, the prelude to more Yoenis Cespedes magic which enabled the Mets to take out the broom.

On the afternoon that the Mets finally clinched the division in Cincinnati, just as Lucas Duda came to the plate in the first inning, I told my listening audience that in the 1969 division clincher, the Mets broke the game open with five first-inning runs (against Carlton and the Cardinals at Shea) on home runs by Donn Clendenon and Ed Charles, and wouldn't it be great to end the suspense early against the Reds? Duda cooperated by hitting a grand slam. Surely this had to mean something special was going on here.

Okay, you want another eerie connection to 1969? Remember one of the low points of the 2015 season? The game they lost in the rain to the San Diego Padres after leading 7–1 at Citi Field probably made you wonder exactly what evil forces were working against the Mets and why? That game was played on July 30. On that very same date forty-six years earlier I was sitting in the left field loge at Shea Stadium as Gil Hodges marched from the dugout to just in front of my friends and me to remove Cleon Jones from the game as the Mets were being walloped in a doubleheader by the Houston Astros. That is widely considered a bottoming out moment for the eventual World Champion Mets of that year.

In the end, despite the chronological similarities, the Mets of 2015 fell three wins short of accomplishing what their 1969 brethren did, but as the T-Shirt says, "The Pennant Will Rise" at Citi Field with the hope that the Mets can complete their unfinished business next season in the manner that the Kansas City Royals did their own on that Sunday night in Flushing. Before that takes place, however, enjoy a far more detailed reflection on the Mets' fifth National League Championship season written by a man who takes each Mets win and loss and finds just the right words to tap into emotions that somehow relate to every fan who reads his work. It's consistently outstanding work, in fact, and this book serves as a wonderful testament. Enjoy the memories, and here's to taking that one final step.

Howie Rose
Broadcaster, New York Mets
WOR Radio, 710 AM
December, 2015

HERE WE GO

OUR PRONOUN OF CHOICE

If you collect baseball cards, yet you don't have one of me, don't fret. Your set is still complete. If you haven't seen me in your official yearbook, no matter how revised the edition, it wasn't a misprint. Fast-forward or rewind through any game you've saved on your DVR. You won't find me in action.

I say this because if you don't know me and start to read what I've written in the pages ahead, you might be confused, because I tend to slip in and out of a certain pronoun of the first-person plural kind.

We. As in we won, we lost, we beat the Nationals, we went into first place, we were going to the playoffs, that sort of thing.

The "we" in question is the New York Mets, a baseball team for whom, as of this writing, 1,007 baseball players have played since April 11, 1962. Chronologically, they encompass everybody from Richie Ashburn to Tim Stauffer (Matt Reynolds, activated without MLB experience during the 2015 postseason, never left the bench, so he's not among them). Alphabetically, they run from David Aardsma through Don Zimmer.

However you track your Mets, you won't find Greg Prince among them. I never could hit, hit with power, pitch, throw or field, not even in my distant youth. I don't think I'd have made much of a holler guy, either, so you can cross "intangibles" off my scouting report.

* * *

What I do for the Mets is root for them. I've been rooting for them virtually my entire life and writing about them on a regular basis for more than a decade. My rooting and writing converge at *Faith and Fear in Flushing*, the blog my friend Jason Fry and I update after every game the Mets play and often when they're at rest.

We say "we" a lot there. It doesn't occur to us not to. Our readers, when they chime in, are prone to "we" as well. Most of those Mets fans I bump into via Facebook, Twitter, and even that app known as real life seem to be on board with our pronoun. When the Mets do something, it's "we" who feel it as much as any Met.

Now and then, someone comes along to scold those of who default to "we" for our use of first-person plural, as if we hadn't noticed we don't dress for games in the Met clubhouse. You're entitled to take these things literally. We don't. We love the Mets too much to spiritually separate ourselves from their ranks. If we could, we wouldn't care enough to be so engaged in their daily doings.

When you read the story that ensues in this volume, you'll be taking it in from the perspective of a highly engaged fan. I've written a couple of other books about the Mets, I've had articles published in various places and I'm very proud of our blog, but don't mistake me for a "sportswriter." I say that with nothing but respect for those who make a living talking to players, watching from press boxes, and banging out copy on deadline. I'm just not one of those people. In case you came here looking for inside information, you'll come away empty. I was watching the 2015 Mets the same way I imagine you were: as a fan who wanted them to win.

That's something they did quite a lot in the year that is the focus of this book, which made me very happy, which will probably be reflected in what you're about to read. This is the story of the first Mets team to win more games than it lost in a season in a while; the first Mets team to extend its season beyond what was initially scheduled in a little while longer; and the first Mets team to earn an invitation to the World Series in quite a long while.

* * *

In the pages of *Amazin' Again*, it is my privilege to process the experience for you as best I can, hopefully bringing to life a journey I doubt we'll soon tire of reliving. Occasionally, I insinuate myself directly into the story.

If I was at a particular game or wish to share a specifically personal obser-
vation, I don't pretend to be detached from the narrative. But this isn't so
much my story as it is the Mets' story . . . which is to say that if you are a
Mets fan like I am a Mets fan, it is *our* story.

Let's go immerse ourselves in it again. And Let's Go Mets.

HOW WE GOT HERE

AN ERA UNWITTINGLY ENDS

Bobby Abreu tipped his cap en route to retirement in the fifth inning. Lucas Duda took a curtain call after belting his 30th home run in the eighth. In the ninth, Jenrry Mejia threw a pitch to L. J. Hoes of the Houston Astros that landed in the glove of Eric Young Jr. for the 27th Houston out of the day and the final box score notation of the season. The New York Mets were 8–3 winners. Time of game was two hours and forty-two minutes.

This was where Met time stood still, or at least hit pause.

At 3:53 p.m. EDT on Sunday, September 28, 2014, in the village of Flushing in the borough of Queens in the City of New York, the 2014 Mets ceased to exist as an active entity. From that moment forward, they'd be a memory, probably the quickly fading kind.

You couldn't blame the 34,897 who held tickets for the last game of the year if they weren't bound to retain much about the team whose victory had just pushed its permanent record to 79–83 and clinched for itself a share of second place in the National League East. Those who came and sat in the Citi Field sun one more time until its playing surface was mostly covered in September shadow might have just been in it for the pleasant afternoon out. That's fair. That's the great thing about baseball. Baseball appeals to a lot of people on a lot of levels. For example, baseball also attracts collectors, and with the Mets distributing Casey Stengel bobbleheads to the first 20,000 through the turnstiles (no matter that they more closely resembled vice principal Woodman from *Welcome Back Kotter* than they did the Ol' Perfesser), there was likely a percentage who paid their way in for the privilege of scooping up the premium.

Sprinkled into the crowd had to be at least a handful of Closing Day aficionados. I know there was one on hand that day, for certain: me. I make it a point to attend the final regularly scheduled home game of every Met season. I appreciate the closure. I relish applauding the Mets who we know we'll never see again, like Abreu, who had announced the previous Friday that this weekend would seal his 18-year career. I revel in the round-number milestones that tend to mark a 162nd game; Duda's 30th homer had me up and out of my seat like a shot. And as for the win itself, well, a win is a win, no matter if it's keeping your team in the race or signifying that the race was run and you rooted for an also-ran.

* * *

If you made it to Citi Field on Sunday, September 28, you could have been there for any number of reasons, but the thrilling conclusion to a dramatic winning season wasn't one of them. The 2014 Mets' version of second place was distant. It was 17 games to the rear of the division champion Washington Nationals, nowhere near a wild card and held in tandem with the recently crumpled Atlanta Braves. The "second-place Mets" had no ring to it. No T-shirts would be printed in their honor, not even by the merchandising masterminds at The 7 Line. Major League Baseball's gradual expansion of postseason eligibility had yet to yield a spot for a 79–83 enterprise.

It was a higher finish and a better record than the Mets had seen for a few years, but it wasn't far removed from the standings and totals the club had been churning out since leaving Shea Stadium and entering Citi Field in 2009. They had yet to win 80 games in a single post-Shea season. They had yet to compete for any prize that wasn't a draft pick in the second half of any year in the 2010s. The decade was half over and the Mets seemed stuck at its beginning. They were 79–83 in 2010. Sandy Alderson and Terry Collins were hired immediately thereafter to improve the ballclub. Four seasons later, they were guiding the Mets to the exact same set of numbers.

For those in attendance on this Closing Day and, really, every Closing Day at Citi Field to date, it appeared the Mets were running in place and walking in circles. Another season ended and the Mets were going a) home and b) nowhere.

Or were they?

* * *

Home, sure. The season was over. But going nowhere? Perhaps the Mets had maintained a maddening consistency across a stretch of sub-.500 seasons, but as long as baseball was ending and you had time enough at last to peruse how the Mets wound up where they did, you could divine hints of progress. At their nadir, the 2014 Mets were 38–49. In their next 75 games, they notched 41 wins. They won more than they lost from the All-Star break onward. From August 29 through September 28, they went 17–11. Again, it was not the stuff of commemorative beer steins, but a different trajectory from that to which we had become miserably accustomed. Usually the hope would tease us in June, only to turn its back on us during some summer-wilting West Coast swing.

This time around, the Mets were getting better as the year got later. They were not yet what you'd call good, but on this Closing Day, once you unpaused and began to mentally fast-forward toward 2015, you could legitimately envision some reasonably exciting coming attractions.

You just couldn't imagine the entirety of what was coming soon.

THE SPIRIT OF '67

There was an old lady, according to a mischievous children's song of yore, who swallowed a fly and, eventually, a creature from virtually every species in a doomed initiative to catch the fly that buzzed around inside her.

That fictional matron had nothing on Bing Devine, general manager of the New York Mets in 1967, the man who set in motion of a chain of events that would have profound impact on the team's fortunes in 2015.

On June 6, 1967, the Mets were working toward constructing an eventual champion. That was the goal, anyway. They didn't know how close they were to achieving it in the late '60s and they certainly had no clue they were laying the foundation for another one that wouldn't emerge for nearly a half-century.

Picturing 2015 back in 1967 was beyond the scope of all but the most ambitious futurologists; for example, who have guessed the Rolling Stones would still be touring 48 years later? In baseball terms, it was tough enough to find a player who you could be reasonably confident would contribute to your ballclub in the not so distant future. The Mets had the first choice in the 1966 draft, and opted for Steve Chilcott over Reggie Jackson. Five-hundred sixty-three home runs later—all of them Jackson's—Cooperstown opted only for Reggie.

No, you can't always get what you want, but Devine was going to try this time to get what the Mets needed with the fourth overall pick in baseball's third-ever June amateur draft. He and the Mets selected a seventeen-year-old left-hander out of West Chester, Pennsylvania, named Jonathan

Trumpbour Matlack. The Mets were barely more than five years old themselves and, to the outside world, light years away from contending. On the day they drafted Matlack, the Mets were holding down tenth place in the National League, a place they finished every year from 1962 through 1965, a place so low it would soon cease to exist.

By the time Matlack made it to the majors to stay, the Mets had already toppled baseball's established order and won a world championship. Nobody had seen those 1969 Mets coming, even if opposing general managers knew Matlack was on his way. He was regularly mentioned as a target in trade talks when the Mets looked into acquiring hitters—talks that went nowhere, given the Mets' fervent belief that young, talented starting pitching is what was going to turn them from pretender to contender. In the wake of the emergence of Tom Seaver, Jerry Koosman, Nolan Ryan, Jim McAndrew, and Gary Gentry, who could argue?

The Mets held on to Matlack. Their judgment was confirmed as wise when he won the NL Rookie of the Year award in 1972 and helped pitch them to a pennant in 1973. He continued to excel despite little run support for several seasons thereafter. At some point, though, with the Mets having reached the end of their run of contention, the club finally relented and traded Matlack—by now a veteran—in their endless quest for any kind of offensive upgrade.

* * *

In December of 1977, the Mets included Matlack in a four-team deal that brought them back three players. The headliner was Willie Montañez, a power-hitting first baseman known for the flair with which he rounded the bases on his occasional home run trots. Willie would give Mets fans a few highlights in an otherwise barren 1978, definitely doing more than one of the other players who came over in that trade, reserve outfielder Tom Grieve. Grieve lasted only that one less than ordinary season (.208/.273/.297) as a Met. Before 1978 could drift into 1979, Tom was swapped to St. Louis in exchange for Brooklyn-born pitcher Pete Falcone.

Falcone had ability but his results were spotty and he was part of a team that was, to put it kindly, perpetually in transition. He made it through four Met seasons before electing free agency. Once Pete signed with the Braves on December 20, 1982, the Mets were granted a compensatory pick in the next June draft, a selection they used on outfielder Stanley Jefferson.

It was Jefferson's misfortune to play center field for an organization whose path to the majors through that position was blocked. Stanley got a taste of champagne as a September call-up in 1986, but he had no chance of dislodging the incumbent center field platoon of Mookie Wilson and Lenny Dykstra. It was no wonder Jefferson became a throw-in to the blockbuster deal that followed the 1986 World Series, the one that sent Kevin Mitchell to San Diego for Kevin McReynolds.

McReynolds could do everything well except exude the kind of passion that differentiated the 1986 Mets from their immediate successors. Still, he was a top-notch player who contributed substantially to the 1988 NL East champs, and the trade that made him a Met looked like a good one . . . until the Mets failed to win another title and Mitchell was rejuvenated after being traded from the Padres to the Giants. When that Kevin earned league MVP honors in 1989, McReynolds's value seemed to dim in New York. Two years later, the Kevin the Mets had to have was shipped to Kansas City in another headline-grabber, this one landing two-time Cy Young awardee Bret Saberhagen.

* * *

Saberhagen had his ups and downs as a Met, but downs were the order of the day in general during his 1992–95 Flushing tenure. The Mets had become one of those teams that looked to shop its big names and salaries at the July trading deadline. Saberhagen went on the market and eventually to the *nouveau-riche* Colorado Rockies. Among the lesser lights obtained by the Mets for Bret was a minor leaguer who never made it to The Show, a pitcher named Arnold Gooch. Gooch rose only as high as Double-A Binghamton until he was folded into a three-way transaction that resulted in speedy Roger Cedeño joining the Mets for the 1999 campaign.

What a season it was for Cedeño, who was taken under the wing of Rickey Henderson and learned to steal bases so well that he set the team record (since broken by Jose Reyes) with 66 thefts. Roger was a key piece of the first Mets playoff team in eleven years and attracted the attention of the Astros in the offseason. Houston had a 22-game winner on its roster, lefty Mike Hampton. Hampton was due a payday. The Astros didn't want to ante up. So a deal was arranged: Cedeño and Octavio Dotel for Hampton and Derek Bell.

Hampton was a rental who turned out to be a fine timeshare. Mike won 15 games as a Met and thoroughly shut down the Cardinals in the 2000 NLCS, taking home series MVP honors. It was a nice prize to pack up and take out the door with him as he pursued free agency and, ultimately, the wonders of greater Denver's public schools. When Colorado signed Hampton away from the Mets, the Mets became entitled to a supplemental first-round pick in the June 2001 draft.

* * *

One day shy of thirty-four years after the Mets grabbed Jon Matlack—who begat a thread that unspooled through Tom Grieve, Pete Falcone, Stan Jefferson, Kevin McReynolds, Bret Saberhagen, Arnie Gooch, Roger Cedeño, and Mike Hampton—a successor to Bing Devine selected an eighteen-year-old third baseman from Chesapeake, Virginia, a high school graduate by the name of David Allen Wright.

The kid was born on December 20, 1982 . . . or the exact same day Falcone signed with the Braves.

The old lady who swallowed a cow to catch the goat to catch the dog to catch the cat to catch the bird to catch the spider to catch the fly couldn't have planned it any more thoroughly or, let's be honest, accidentally. Met management across multiple generations was just trying to improve its team in the here and now. What GMs Devine (the Matlack selection), Joe McDonald (the trades for Grieve and Falcone), Frank Cashen (the drafting of Jefferson, the trade for McReynolds), Al Harazin (the Saberhagen acquisition), Joe McIlvaine (picking up Gooch), and

Steve Phillips (getting Cedeño, then Hampton, then making the fateful pick of Wright) wound up conspiring to accomplish was the cementing of the cornerstone of a National League champion. The championship wouldn't be achieved until some very far off year, but everything has to start somewhere.

Nobody knew it any better on June 5, 2001, than they could have on June 6, 1967, but the day David Wright was drafted by the New York Mets was the day the first mile marker along the road to the 2015 World Series was driven solidly into the franchise's terra firma.

WRIGHT HERE, WRIGHT STILL

David Wright lived a charmed baseball life. He was born and raised in the Tidewater region of Virginia, which as any Mets fan with a memory can tell you was where just about every Met minor leaguer of note played before making the majors between 1969 and 2006. David's proximity to the Tidewater and later Norfolk Tides made him a Mets fan growing up. His swift progress through the system, topping out as a Triple-A Tide, made him a Met by the age of twenty-one. He broke in on July 21, 2004, for a faltering Mets club that desperately needed a boost. The Mets kept faltering, but David was on the rise from the moment he showed up at Shea. In 69 games as a rookie, the young third baseman hit .293 and homered 14 times.

Things only got better in 2005, when his OPS measured .912 and his bare hand pulled in a pop fly in the sort of play that makes an athlete a *SportsCenter* staple. The Mets improved as a team in 2005 and then emerged in a significant fashion in 2006, winning a division title and reaching the seventh game of the National League Championship Series. The kid who wore No. 5 was rapidly becoming the No. 1 attraction in Queens, having made his first All-Star team in '06 and finishing ninth in MVP voting.

Thereafter, David Wright's baseball life grew less and less charmed.

* * *

Individually, he put together a pair of dynamite individual seasons, but the Mets of 2007 and 2008 injected "collapse" into their fans' vocabularies in each of those Septembers. The club moved to their new ballpark, Citi Field, in 2009, a facility that was friendlier to the Brooklyn Dodger legacy than it was Wright's opposite-field power. No Met hit many home runs at home in '09, but the drought was most noticeable for David, whose overall tater total tumbled from 33 to 10. Also, for his trouble, he went on the disabled list for the first time in his career after an accidental beaning from the Giants' Matt Cain. Meanwhile, the Mets cut out the collapsing middleman by simply ceasing to contend.

David would craft some representative numbers in the seasons ahead and be mightily appreciated for his labors. The respectful young man who not long before embodied a bright Met future in tandem with shortstop Jose Reyes grew into the clear leader of a ballclub in search of itself. Whereas Reyes was allowed to leave as a free agent after winning a batting title in 2011, Wright was signed to an extremely long-term deal, essentially guaranteeing he'd play his entire presumably lengthy career as a New York Met, an act of Metropolitan endurance essentially nobody not named Ed Kranepool or Ron Hodges could claim.

Wright also had bestowed on him the title of captain entering the 2013 season, a fitting responsibility for a player who'd put himself out front for a franchise that had spent years otherwise rattling around in a fit of sustained futility. When things went well for the team, the media flocked to David's locker for an analysis. When things went awry (as they tended to do), he wore the de facto designation—per President Obama's description of former President Clinton—of explainer-in-chief.

After one of those seasons when hope crumbled late, David would stoically pronounce, "It's obviously painful" or "We failed as a team." When the Mets would gather again and the odds looked long, David would display his stiffest upper lip: "We're expecting to go out there and win the National League East and go deep in the playoffs and win the World Series." And when that didn't happen? "At the end of the day," he'd admit, "it's tough to really enjoy anything [when] we . . . don't make the playoffs again."

In his first decade on the job, Wright made seven All-Star teams, a Met total matched only by Darryl Strawberry and surpassed only by Tom Seaver. He picked up a couple of Gold Gloves. He finished as high as fourth in MVP balloting. He was dubbed "Captain America" for his efforts on behalf of Team USA in the World Baseball Classic and generated enough support among Mets fans to be voted the Face of MLB, a rather silly Twitter exercise, but one reflective of Mets-lovers' loyalty to their main man.

* * *

"Forever" was a perilous term for a franchise that twice let Seaver—a.k.a. The Franchise—leave its premises, but David Wright was going to be a Met forever. From 2004 to eternity was a long road, but you somehow knew or at least hoped that when the Mets made themselves playoff-eligible again, the Captain would be at the heart of it.

For all that goodwill, Wright wasn't getting any younger or healthier. He'd missed time in 2011 due to a back injury and again in 2013 (hamstring) and 2014 (shoulder). For that matter, the Mets weren't getting any better if you viewed their progress through the prism of winning more than they lost. When he signed the contract that would keep him a Met through 2020, David swore he was assured by Sandy Alderson and Jeff Wilpon that help was on its way. In his earlier years, he played alongside Mike Piazza, Tom Glavine, Cliff Floyd, Pedro Martinez, Carlos Beltran, Carlos Delgado, Paul Lo Duca, Billy Wagner, and Johan Santana. Now *that* was what you could call help, even if they only helped so much for so long. The Mets weren't bringing in that stratum of established talent any longer, not in the post-Bernie Madoff reality in which ownership was trying to do business. The bulk of the talent Wright was convinced was coming was going to have to rise like he did, from the Mets' farm system.

Were the Mets really growing something special down there? Or was all the talk David was dying to believe the baseball equivalent of a load of fertilizer?

SUCCESS HAS TWO DADDIES

Success, it is said, has many fathers, but failure is an orphan. The 2015 Mets, you might say, had two daddies. DNA testing was in the eye of the beholder. There was the GM who made all the right personnel moves and there was the GM who reaped more than his share of kudos for the other guy's vision.

Ah, but which was which? Sandy Alderson had been Generally Managing the Mets since the fall of 2010, taking over for the generally disparaged Omar Minaya. The Mets became, in the books where this information is inscribed, Sandy's team.

Yet, where would have Sandy's team have been without Omar's players? There was, naturally, a passel of holdovers on the Mets' organizational depth chart when Sandy took over. Some who tired of waiting for Alderson to weave his alleged magic wished to make the case for Minaya as prophet without honor in bequeathing his successor a richly stocked pool of potential. Say what you will, they said, but you can't say Omar didn't recognize talent. When some young Mets began to impress, it seemed worth noting they were the products of Minaya's due diligence

At odds with this worldview was a contingent that believed Alderson was exactly what the Mets needed because Minaya left the franchise in such shoddy shape, thus requiring Sandy's steady guidance and copious amounts of time for him to undo Omar's damage. The sense from this perspective was Minaya was an adequate GM when he had a mandate to act impulsively and a barrel of Madoff money to throw at somebody else's stars. When his approach didn't yield immediate results (and after a while it unquestionably didn't), Omar could never quite explain himself satisfactorily, making the calm, cool, sabermetrically inclined bearing of Alderson's front office a necessary balm for a wounded baseball operation.

There you had it: two versions of essentially the same situation, perfect fodder for one of those flashback-heavy episodes of *The Odd Couple* in which Oscar is the righteously aggrieved party until Felix gets his turn to tell the tale.

* * *

I thought the hindsight-laden attempt to assign definitive credit and blame was a bizarre parlor game for Mets fans to indulge in. Cable news channels traffic in black and white. Orange and blue is far more complex than grimy partisan politics. True, you have to fill up the hours between the last pitch last night and the first pitch tonight, but slagging Minaya/Alderson just so you can ladle additional praise on Alderson/Minaya? How about being happy that you're happy with the players you've got, however they got here?

At the time of Omar Minaya's unmourned departure from New York, seven 2015 Mets to be—besides David Wright, who was drafted and signed by Steve Phillips—had already bowed for the big club; four of them would prove themselves April-to-autumn mainstays when '15 rolled around. By the end of the 2010 season, a dozen eventual members of the 2015 squad were in the minors, most prominent among them the core of their starting rotation, their usually lockdown closer, and the infielder who'd become their emotional avatar.

In the spring of 2011, when the first Alderson team was fielding the likes of Brad Emaus, Blaine Boyer, and Chin-lung Hu, you wouldn't have necessarily skimmed a list that included names like Steven Matz, Jacob deGrom, Jeurys Familia, and Wilmer Flores and automatically frothed with anticipation that a surefire pennant-winner was being built.

Yet a nucleus was forming. It was a long way from being formed, but some of the pieces were, if not in place, at least in the box. The Mets had Daniel Murphy, Jon Niese, Ruben Tejada, and Lucas Duda at the major league level. They were developing Matt Harvey, Minaya's final No. 1 draft pick in 2010, while figuring out what they had in the other young pitchers and players already on hand.

* * *

The rest of the job fell to Alderson and his crew. They did the developing, the shepherding, and the nurturing while making moves of their own. Perhaps no Minaya legacy was greater than that attached to R. A. Dickey, a classic scrap heap find. Omar picked up an end-of-the-line knuckleballer who transformed into a phenomenon, folk hero, and 2012 Cy Young winner. By the time R. A. became a Met icon, Omar was long gone.

Alderson traded the hyperliterate legend. It was one of those moves that was uncomfortable to reckon in the moment, yet widely understood as having been done for the good of the future. Dickey, adored by Mets fans, was sent to Toronto at the peak of his value for a shipment of promising prospects, primarily catcher Travis d'Arnaud and pitcher Noah Syndergaard. The Mets had lacked a genuine long-term presence behind the plate since the days of Mike Piazza, so a catcher with a future was a must-get. As for pitching, you could never have too much of that, and Syndergaard's right arm was considered as golden as any in the sport, right up there with those belonging to Harvey and Zack Wheeler, another highly coveted pitcher Alderson nabbed on the way up (from San Francisco for the expiring contract of Carlos Beltran in the summer of '11).

The Hus and Emauses were giving way to a different kind of free agent by 2014. Alderson wasn't authorized to throw nine-figure pacts around, but he did invest in a couple of veterans who had been playoff participants and knew a little something about playing in New York (albeit on the other side of town). In came Curtis Granderson to play right field and Bartolo Colon to take the starts that would pile up while Harvey rehabilitated from Tommy John surgery. Each persevered across the '14 campaign and contributed to the Mets' late rise to the cusp of .500.

Another vet in the same "professional" mold, Rockies outfielder Michael Cuddyer, was lured to Queens in advance of 2015, inking his two-year deal at an authentically auspicious Met moment. The Mets were willing to forfeit to Colorado a first-round draft pick—perhaps karmic compensation for plucking Wright, who happened to be an old Virginia buddy of Cuddyer's—to secure the services of the 2013 NL batting champ. Two years earlier, when Michael Bourn loomed as an alluring answer in center field, the Mets wouldn't choose today over tomorrow (that was the offseason when Alderson stood before the annual baseball writers' dinner, shrugged at his lack of immediate options and impishly asked, "what outfield?"). The arrival of tomorrow had a funny way of inevitably getting stuck in traffic.

Tomorrow, however, could finally be spotted exiting the Grand Central and pulling into the Citi Field parking lot. The Mets let their No. 1 pick for June 2015 go in the interest of securing what they judged a dependable bat for the present. For his part, Michael insisted he decided to come to the Mets because he thought they had a genuine chance to win—now.

* * *

Every free agent says something like that about the team whose dollars he's graciously accepting, but Cuddyer's November 2014 affirmation carried the tinge of truth. Duda's surge to 30 homers and 92 RBIs was still fresh in the mind's eye. Juan Lagares, yet another of Minaya's slow-burn minor leaguers, exploded into the baseball consciousness and was voted a Gold Glove for his otherworldly defensive wizardry in center, having long before made the Bourn flirtation moot. On the very day news of Cuddyer's signing broke, deGrom was named the winner of the NL Rookie of the Year award. Familia and d'Arnaud each gathered token support in the balloting as well. Most encouraging of all, Harvey was going to pitch again when the Mets, like the swallows to Capistrano, returned to Port St. Lucie in February. All of these players Cuddyer was so anxious to join forces with were scouted and signed by the old regime . . . and grew to flourish in the new regime.

The best of two worlds seemed to be meshing. Point to Minaya's machinations as the main reason? Thank goodness exclusively for Alderson's applications? If the work of each GM contributed to a Met winner, it wouldn't occur to a supremely satisfied Mets fan to bother asking.

HOW WE GOT GOING

HOPE SPRINGS FITFULLY

S pring training exists for one reason where fans are concerned. It's there to excite us beyond reason. Nothing much happens, and that's all right. We don't need much. We used to get by with a string of elliptical non sequiturs in the daily paper and we loved it.

*Doug Flynn is experimenting with a heavier bat.... **Kevin Kobel** is working on a sinker.... The club announced Fireworks Night will be in June....**Joe Torre** promised **Dwight Bernard** will get a long look for a relief role.... A noticeably trimmer **Dan Norman** arrived 10 pounds lighter, owing his weight loss to cutting back on potatoes.... Traveling secretary **Lou Niss** was bundled up against a particularly stiff wind during the morning workout.... **Elliott Maddox** and **Lee Mazzilli** are getting over colds.*

Slap a "ST. PETERSBURG, Fla." dateline in front of it, maybe add a few paragraphs on how this is going to be the year for Pete Falcone, and we were set.

Nowadays, spring training is covered by a dragnet of seriously purposed journalists, all of whom are armed with Twitter accounts, none of whom, presumably, wants his or her expense account questioned. It tends to lead to information overload, leading me to one inviolable perennial conclusion on what to look for as our Mets prepare for their season:

Nothing.

No news is good news.

* * *

If I come across anything resembling substance, I worry. For example, when I read rookie Noah Syndergaard raised the ire of veterans David Wright and Bobby Parnell because he dared to eat lunch in the clubhouse during an intrasquad game—twenty-two and 6'6", the boy was hungry, for goodness sake—I realized instinctively it was nothing (unless it could be pointed to retroactively as a rallying point for an unforeseen run to the World Series). I worried nonetheless. The last thing I want out of spring training news is actual spring training news.

Tyler Pill wasn't spring training news when spring training commenced and once he was reassigned to minor league camp, he was promptly forgotten in the scheme of the 2015 Mets. But the appearance of this rookie righty, less celebrated than Syndergaard, turned out to be a canary in a coal mine for the first substantive news to emanate north from Port St. Lucie. Pill was starting a meaningless exhibition game televised back to New York on March 14. The game remained meaningless. Its ultimate meaning was embedded in the presence of Pill.

Zack Wheeler was supposed to start that game. He was scratched. *No big deal* was the word from the Mets (dutifully repeated and retweeted ASAP). You wanted to believe that was true. You didn't want to be a pill just because you saw Pill. But you were a Mets fan who lived through a decade of misdiagnosed Met injuries that generally erred on the side of overoptimistic when it came to how serious they were and how long they'd take to get over. Never mind Ty. What was up with Zack, the starting pitcher who was slated to be a cornerstone of the rotation intended to spin the Mets into contention at last?

Maybe it really was nothing. Or maybe it would follow the usual trajectory of the Mets' injury pronouncements.

He's not going to throw today as scheduled.
He's fine, just a little dead-arm period.
They're taking precautions, just normal stiffness.
He'll be throwing again in a day or two.
He's not making the trip to Viera, but that shouldn't cause any alarms.
He says he feels "100%," but they're going to wait.

It might be nothing more than he slept on it wrong.
He may have experienced a slight setback.
Just to be careful, they're going to send him for an MRI.
The way the schedule is set up, they can go without an extra arm until late April.
They're going to have him consult with Dr. Andrews, but that's fairly standard procedure.
He's going to try rehabilitation without surgery.
Surgery was successful.
He should be ready to resume baseball activities before the All-Star break.
He'll be reporting to St. Lucie by August 1.
There's a chance we'll see him when the rosters expand in September.
The Mets haven't yet announced whether they will wear a patch in his memory in 2016.

Wheeler survived the season ahead but he never did make it back to a major league mound. Tommy John surgery—the same scourge that claimed Matt Harvey when he was all we had and Jacob deGrom before any of us knew who he was—was in his right elbow's immediate future. The Mets' near term would not include Wheeler, whose steady progress through 2014 was cause for genuine optimism. They would also be without two bullpen specialists they'd been counting on: Josh Edgin (TJS on his left elbow) and Vic Black (weak right shoulder). The three promising young pitchers combined for zero appearances for the 2015 Mets.

Losing a trio of heretofore live arms didn't noticeably slow the Mets in their march toward April. No Grapefruit League team won more games (19) than the Mets. They didn't matter in the standings, but were they meaningless? Was momentum something you could ship up I-95 on the equipment truck? Wasn't momentum regularly identified as your next day's starting pitcher?

On the next day that a Mets game would matter, they would start a pitcher who'd been pitching professionally when toddler Noah Syndergaard was just getting acquainted with solid food.

OPENING DAYS

All teams' fans embrace Opening Day. Mets fans probably hug it a little harder than most. Never mind the secular holiday aspect. Never mind the blades of grass and the sun's return and the sense that we made it through one more winter only slightly scathed. That's great, too, but the reason we are fiercely proprietary of Opening Day above all days is that's the day we win. Not the only day we win, but the day we've come to expect to win. It's not our imagination. After going 0-for-the-1960s, the Mets have practically owned Opening Day, winning with satisfying frequency: 21–4 between 1970 and 1994; 10–3 from 2001 to 2013; 34 of 45 overall heading into 2015. Even in 1981, when the strike-ruptured split season demanded a Reopening Day in August, the Mets won that, too.

All the adages add up in the Mets' favor where not losing lidlifters is concerned. Good pitching beats good hitting. The pitchers are ahead of the hitters early on. You can't hit what you don't see. The Mets have sent aces on the level of Tom Seaver (11 times), Dwight Gooden (8), and Johan Santana (4) to throw the very first pitches of their seasons, which might explain their traditional advantages on Opening Day. You have aces, you deal aces. The Mets, it was agreed on the eve of 2015, had at least two indisputable aces: Matt Harvey, the starter for the 2013 National League All-Star team, and Jacob deGrom, the winner of the 2014 National League Rookie of the Year award. Both were young, both were strong, and both were primed and ready to go.

* * *

So Terry Collins handed the ball to Bartolo Colon, who you could have mistaken for the guy disinterestedly passing somebody else's hot dog money to the vendor at the end of your row . . . and maybe deciding to order a couple for himself. Colon wasn't without credentials, having made his professional debut in 1994 and having pitched successfully and occasionally brilliantly in the big leagues since 1997, but he didn't appear deGrom- let alone Dark Knight-caliber at this stage of his career. Colon finished 2014, his first year as a Met, as you might expect a forty-one-year-old would. He ate up innings (such a straight line) but didn't always devour hitters. The future was allegedly about Matt and Jake, with Noah coming along soon.

Bartolo Colon was going to start on Opening Day in Washington? What, I wondered— were Mike Torrez and Pete Harnsich not available? Terry Collins, it was easy to conclude, didn't quite know he was doing. It wouldn't be the last time a Mets fan would question the handle he had on his personnel and it wouldn't be the last time the questioner would come away realizing this Collins guy might know his personnel better than he did.

I wanted Harvey or deGrom out there. I settled for Colon. I got more than I deserved, given my underestimation of Bartolo. Against the consensus-favorite Nationals, Colon shone. Washington had won the NL East the year before somewhat on the backs of the Mets, beating them 15 out of 19 times, absolutely demolishing them at Citi Field, while merely brushing them aside at Nationals Park. They'd made themselves even better with the expensive addition of erstwhile American League Cy Young winner Max Scherzer. They were loaded with pitching, hitting, and confidence.

* * *

Yet they lost to Bartolo Colon and the Mets, 3–1, evidence of the need to play the games, let alone the season, before deciding what's going to happen. If you wanted proof that nobody knows anything in advance, Colon earning the W and Scherzer being saddled with the L didn't necessarily constitute necessarily Exhibit A. That honor could have been bestowed on where the S was found in the box score.

The save on Opening Day went to Buddy Carlyle. Buddy—a member of MLB rosters on and off since 1999, but not until 2015 a pitcher in any season's first game—wasn't suddenly designated closer by Collins in another fit of overwhelming trust in veteran experience. He wanted to use Jenrry Mejia. Mejia had nailed down 28 saves in 2014. The formula was Jeurys Familia for the eighth (three Nats faced, three Nats retired), Mejia for the ninth. But Terry's call to the bullpen yielded word that Jenrry's elbow wasn't quite right. Hence, the ninth inning became one-third Jerry Blevins, the former National lefty acquired late in spring, and two-thirds Carlyle.

Bartolo, Blevins, and Buddy. Sounds like a pilot ABC passed on, but it gave the Mets all the momentum they needed to keep their Opening Day tradition intact: 35–11 since 1970, 1–0 in 2015.

* * *

The next game's starter was deGrom. He pitched well, but the Mets were edged. The day after that was the first Harvey Day since August 24, 2013. This was a festival of hope and heat celebrated by Mets fans every fifth day two years earlier. The party had been put on hold while Matt rehabilitated his valuable right elbow, sometimes under a little brighter and more self-generated spotlight than his employers preferred. Harvey, however, was the heir to the ace tradition. Seaver to Gooden to a detour through some high-priced imports to, at last, a homegrown starter you could imagine taking the ball for the first game for seasons to come . . . maybe even for the first game of a World Series to come.

Matt Harvey returned triumphantly, defeating Stephen Strasburg and the Nationals with six innings of nine-strikeout shutout ball. In April of '13, when the two youngsters faced off at Citi Field, the Mets starter outclassed his then better-known opponent, inspiring a spontaneous chant of "HARVEY'S BETTER!" It may have been the first original positive sentiment to have been born at the brick-laden ballpark. Four months later, Harvey was on the sidelines. Now he was back and seemingly in full Knighthood. Strasburg hadn't really been the same since his own Tommy John surgery in 2010. It was tough to expect any pitcher to rebound quickly or fully from a procedure in which his ulnar collateral ligament is replaced.

Not that that appeared to be a worry for the Dark Knight on the afternoon of April 9. He was a superhero. We were sure of it.

The Mets left Washington having trumped the Nationals in their first series of the year, sending a Bat signal of sorts that they were not to be taken lightly in the year ahead. But almost as soon as the team arrived in Atlanta, they realized only a joker would believe their journey would be obstacle-free. Mejia's problem elbow was only the second-most troubling aspect of his nascent 2015. The Mets announced that Jenrry was suspended for the next 80 games in accordance with Major League Baseball's policy on PEDs. Mejia was found to have taken Stanozolol. It was described as an old-school steroid, but for Mets fans, the name wasn't crucial to learn; it could have been Stan Musial. All they knew was they were without their closer. Their next viable option and Mejia's predecessor, Bobby Parnell, was still working his way back from the injury that caused him to miss the vast majority of 2014.

Familia, he of the solid eighth innings, was moving up. He would take the ninth from now on. As for the Mets, they would take a couple of lumps in Atlanta, losing twice before salvaging the finale. They were headed home with a 3–3 record and no obvious momentum behind it.

The next day would change that feeling altogether.

THIS FELT DIFFERENT

Flushing was sunny and bright as it welcomed its Mets to 2015. Sunny and bright should be the default atmosphere for every home opener. In 2014, snow fell over the metropolitan area on the late-March morning the Mets prepared to commence their season. Not a lot, but enough to be atonal. The precipitation evaporated by the time the first game was over, but so did a ninth-inning Mets lead.

Better weather and better omens greeted this year's version on April 13. Jacob deGrom beat the Phillies, 2–0, as Citi Field made previously unfathomable amounts of noise in support. The Mets had cobbled together their first winning streak of the season, a modest two games, but it was something to build on.

One night later, Matt Harvey was again the center of attention, though there were several events competing for notice among the nearly 40,000 on hand who'd been waiting twenty months to volubly salute the Dark Knight. The Phillies were a shadow of their heretofore champion selves, but one of their old warhorses, Chase Utley, had stuck around and he was still sticking it to the Mets. The former All-Star second baseman smacked two homers and drove in another run with a single *and* managed to be in the middle of some serious chippiness as Harvey buried a pitch in his back as unstated retaliation for the Phillie starter, David Buchanan, having already plunked two Mets.

Utley wasn't popular with the Citi Field crowd as the season settled in. A crystal ball couldn't have told you how he'd be thought of much later in 2015.

Mixed in amid Harvey's return and the HBP drama was a catcher's interference call against Travis d'Arnaud, an ejection of Terry Collins stemming from his vehement protest of the call, a replay challenge of a play at the plate by Phillies manager Ryne Sandberg that went in the Mets' favor and the third base debut of Anthony Recker, career backup catcher. Recker became the 154th third baseman in Mets history— joining the long line of luminaries that includes Sammy Drake (8th), Joe Moock (35th), Jack Heidemann (49th), and Phil Mankowski (64th)—when David Wright (No. 129) pulled his right hamstring while stealing second in the eighth inning. It wasn't thought Wright would be out for long.

What was known for sure was Harvey was a winner once more, as the Mets, half of their bullpen, and all of their bench held off their old rivals, 6–5, for a third consecutive victory. When Jon Niese and the two unrelated Torreses—stalwart righty Carlos, recently acquired lefty Alex—disposed of Philadelphia the next night, the Mets had themselves their first series sweep of the year and a four-game winning streak.

* * *

Into Citi Field swam the Marlins, nemeses of a different nature. The Marlins, no Mets fan needed reminding, tripped up their team en route to the playoffs in 2007 and 2008. They represented the final peg in the ladders of collapses past. And even when little was on the line, they were the Marlins. They were always finding a way to ruin the Mets' lives.

Despite their perceived nettlesomeness and despite the ever discomfiting presence of slugger Giancarlo Stanton, the Marlins were fish out of water off Flushing Bay this mid-April. Miami came in for four and left with none. Another Mets sweep, extending their winning streak to eight. The standings, such as they could be after two weeks, made for alluring reading. The first-place Mets already edged second-place Atlanta by a game-and-a-half and were four up on the Nats.

Less tangible but somehow just as real was the feeling that surrounded these suddenly unbeatable Mets. Call it a spiritual rebirth, a renewal of faith, a New York state of enlightenment. Call it going into a game with the sense that your team is more likely to win than lose, that the burden of suck was on the other guys now. Somewhere between sweeping the Phillies and sweeping the Marlins arose a feeling that the Mets had swept away their frustrating recent past.

The mold was broken. The streak stayed intact.

The wins over Miami—7–5, 4–1, 5–4, 7–6—carried with them a brand of steely determination we weren't used to. The 7 Line, the apparel entrepreneurs who knew how to tap into the Mets fan psyche and illustrate it on wearable fabric, had over the winter recreated a thirty-five-year-old T-shirt that said "The Magic is Back," an echo of the 1980 Mets' ad campaign that resonated through the years because it spoke to a central Met myth. If the club was defeating expectations, the stars must be aligning, the underdogs must be howling and Steve Henderson must be coming to bat in the bottom of the ninth, the Mets down by two with two out after seeming to be completely out of it just a couple of minutes ago.

The "Magic" lovingly recalled from that era didn't last more than a summer, but the high points always made for a helluva story (Henderson homered to complete a remarkable Saturday night comeback at its apex). The new version of the shirt proved popular, but applying its ethos to 2015 didn't quite fit. This wasn't magic the Mets were relying on to punch up in their division. They broke through by playing good, solid baseball in every facet of the game and grabbed immediate hold of first place as a result. We weren't coming home from yet another Mets win at Citi Field in April breathlessly telling anybody who'd listen how the Mets pulled one out. These Mets didn't have to pull anything out. They were playing like the better team across nine innings. They *were* the better team. The old ballpark victory song had been replaced this year by Ace Frehely's "New York Groove," but really, as April unfolded, this was a Bachman Turner Overdrive kind of team.

They were takin' care of business every day.

* * *

Even without Wright (still not back from that hamstring pull). Even without—by the end of the Marlin series—d'Arnaud and Jerry Blevins, victims of a pitch off the hand and a liner off the arm, respectively. Individual Mets were dropping even as the collective unit was rising.

The ascension continued with Atlanta's arrival into Citi Field. After using the same lineup in six of the season's first eight games, Collins would be forced to vamp for a mighty long stretch (the Opening Day octet that supported Bartolo Colon in Washington wouldn't take the field together again in 2015 after April 14). Kevin Plawecki filled in for d'Arnaud. Hansel Robles replaced Blevins in the bullpen. Along the bottom line, nothing changed. The Mets beat the Braves once . . . twice . . . thrice. On the blustery afternoon of April 23, the Mets completed a sweep of yet another old burr in their saddle. The numbers now were staggering.

- A 13–3 start, matching the Mets' sprint from the 1986 gate, and catapulting them as far above .500 as they'd been in any season since a too-brief spurt in the middle of 2010.
- A perfect 10–0 homestand, totally unprecedented in franchise annals.
- An overall 11-game winning streak, equal to the mark set in 1969 and tied in 1972, 1986, and 1990. Two of those outfits were extraordinarily special in Met lore. None of them produced a losing record.
- A four-and-a-half-game lead over second-place Atlanta and, more relevantly, a six-game spread ahead of Washington, the supposed surefire division winners.

The reality of the National League East, much like the feeling of relentlessly joyous Citi Field, was different. A long way remained until October— the final 146 games of a baseball season are often the hardest—but the sour times that had hovered over two different ballparks across the previous eight years had at last blown out to sea.

HOW WE GOT STUCK

WHAT'S SPINAL STENOSIS?

The only thing better than possibly breaking the franchise consecutive games won record would have been to break it against the Yankees, who the Mets were seeing unusually early in 2015. Alas, the streak was snapped before it could get to 12, as the Mets fell in the Bronx on April 24 and ruined their chances to finish 159–3. Matt Harvey turned the tables the next afternoon, leading the way to an 8–2 win that featured a Flushing fusillade. Home runs were hit by Lucas Duda, Kevin Plawecki (his first ever), and Eric "Soup" Campbell, subbing for the still absent David Wright. The NBA Nets and NHL Islanders each won playoff games on the same Saturday. New York could be forgiven its simmering case of postseason fever, current and projected.

The Mets would lose the Subway Series but put it behind them quickly, scoring a dramatic victory on their next out-of-town road date, when Daniel Murphy unloaded a ninth-inning three-run homer off Steve Cishek to prevail at Marlins Park, 3–1. The first-place Mets now led the last-place Nationals by eight games.

So maybe the Magic was a little bit Back.

Just when things couldn't get any better for these 2015 Mets . . . they didn't. Baseball seasons are like that. The 1969 Mets fell off the miraculous pace they set from May to July. The 1986 Mets lost a third of their games. This edition would encounter more adversity and begin to be affected by it.

* * *

The impact of losing Wright (hitting .333), Travis d'Arnaud (.317), and Jerry Blevins (15 batters faced, 15 batters retired) couldn't help but eventually ripple through the roster. The aches and pains were almost contagious. Second base prospect Dilson Herrera was called up only to go on the disabled list two weeks later. Relievers Rafael Montero and Buddy Carlyle each went down with injuries, never to return in 2015. Dillon Gee, who'd been pitching quietly and generally consistently since 2010, landed on the DL on May 9 after straining his right groin.

It was the strain heard round the Met world, or at least clear to Triple-A Las Vegas, where the Mets used the unfortunate development as opportunity to summon Thor.

Mets fans had been waiting to welcome Noah Syndergaard from the moment he was acquired in the R.A. Dickey trade. The idea that fueled the Dickey trade of December 2012 was that someday it would be known as the Syndergaard trade. It had already shown signs of tilting the Mets' way. R. A., who had just been crowned NL Cy Young winner, was shipped to Toronto at the peak of his prowess and popularity. Prominent among the four players received was d'Arnaud, potentially the kind of starting catcher we'd lacked since the fleeting Met heyday of Paul Lo Duca (or maybe Mike Piazza, if we were really lucky). Yet Travis was considered the secondary piece in the Canadian bounty that somehow cleared customs and immediately bolstered the Met farm system. Syndergaard was the most glittering lure.

Dickey wasn't likely going to get any better than he'd been for us in 2012. Syndergaard—tall, fast and nicknamed in advance—was going to be as good as anybody for a long time to come. That was the word. Mets fans, never voted Most Patient in any league-wide survey, had been panting for a long look at the young man in action.

We got it on May 12 as Noah debuted at Wrigley Field. He was clearly capable and emitted veritable flashes of lightning in a loss to the Cubs, which was part of an otherwise discouraging Chicago sweep. Thor made his Citi Field debut on May 17, the afternoon after the Mets exploded for an uncharacteristic 10-run inning against Milwaukee. Fans were already dressed in comic book gear and didn't feel silly afterwards when the rookie hammered home his first win, a 5–1 decision that kept the Mets afloat. Their eight-game bulge over Washington had dwindled to a slim half-game.

* * *

First place became a memory a couple of days later, as the inevitable Nationals surged past New York in historically disconcerting fashion. In the Mets' five previous division-winning seasons, once the team had settled into first place, they never vacated the top spot. In all other seasons, letting go meant saying goodbye. Oh well, one could rationalize, we all knew Washington was stacked and there's always the wild card.

"Always," however, was revealing itself a shaky Metropolitan proposition. The Mets, it seemed, had always had David Wright at third base. He was the player who had halted once and for all the spin of the hot corner revolving door upon his July 21, 2004, debut. Maybe it was ancient history by then, but the Mets had spent most of their first two decades searching for one man to play third base and play it well one year after another. There had been some fine albeit transitory Met third basemen before David Wright; with David Wright entrenched, Mets fans didn't have to wonder in the slightest about who was on third.

He made multiple All-Star teams as the Mets grew into contenders and even when they grew out of contending. He owned the upper echelons of the Met record book and earned the captaincy. He symbolized stability in the face of flux. David was under contract through 2020. You couldn't get more eternal than that.

Eternity, however, was put on pause on May 23 as it was announced in Pittsburgh that Wright, working his way back from that April hamstring strain, was having back trouble. Enormous back trouble. Something called spinal stenosis. Every Mets fan who never went to medical school sought to become an instant authority. What we learned collectively was:

a) Spinal stenosis meant the cavity in the middle of Wright's lower back had narrowed.
b) There were no ready examples of athletes who picked up their careers where they left off once they were diagnosed with it—and several whose time on the field was severely curtailed or essentially over when they were found to be afflicted by it.

c) The key Met of the previous decade and the Met who was supposed to play a key role in unlocking the hopes of 2015 was not coming back soon, perhaps not coming back ever.

The entire situation had to be filed under "Who knows?" In the weeks ahead, the same question would be asked as answer to another pressing question:

Are the Mets ever going to score again?

THE PITCHERS DO IT ALL

This Thor kid really got your attention. The outsize frame, the long blonde locks, the 100 MPH fastballs—and he could hit. On May 27, Noah Syndergaard drove a Sean O'Sullivan pitch over Citi Field's center field wall, raising the Home Run Apple and, in time-honored National League fashion, helping his own cause as the Mets completed a sweep over the ragtag Phillies. Any plate appearance that ends in a pitcher circling the bases is noteworthy. For Mets fans, Syndergaard's slugging was really something to savor.

The Mets needed hitters. It didn't matter what position they played. Jacob deGrom, Matt Harvey, and Jon Niese could each handle a bat. Bartolo Colon, unathletic appearance notwithstanding, worked to make himself a serviceable hitting pitcher (still not good, but no longer a guaranteed out). Syndergaard had raked in Vegas and now he was flexing his muscles in the majors.

Not a lot of other Mets were. Lighting up the Quadruple-A Phillies staff wasn't tough, but as the Mets approached June and took on more daunting opposition, they had to wonder where their bats went.

It wasn't like their starting eight were seen using them.

* * *

The pitchers were pitching very well. The pitchers were pitching in with their hitting (Terry Collins batted his starter eighth 25 times in 2015). The hitters were missing in action. It was understandable, to a certain extent.

You don't lose David Wright and Travis d'Arnaud and not feel it. Same for Daniel Murphy, when a quad strain sidelined him in early June. But the void these Mets left threatened to swallow whole what had been such a promising season.

Soup Campbell was no Captain. Kevin Plawecki, a former first-round draft pick, was not yet in the class of d'Arnaud. They were struggling. So was John Mayberry Jr., an offseason pickup who didn't live up to his slight track record. So was Michael Cuddyer, free agent left fielder who performed sleight-of-hand tricks in the clubhouse but otherwise conjured memories of the shortcomings of Jason Bay. Wilmer Flores was still learning everyday-playing on the job; Lucas Duda wasn't quite following up on his breakout 2014; Juan Lagares, held back in part by a bad elbow, had regressed in all aspects of his game; and Curtis Granderson was getting by mainly on walks and charm. Ruben Tejada, so often dismissed as offensively inadequate, was, on the strength of an uncharacteristically good week and change, the team's hottest hitter.

The miasma of the Met offense culminated on the night of June 9 at Citi Field, when rookie Chris Heston started for the Giants and held the Mets scoreless, hitless, and hopeless. It was the first no-hitter thrown at the Mets since Darryl Kile did it to a much worse outfit in 1993; heretofore hot-hitting Tejada took called strike three to end it. In the scheme of things, the no-no didn't have to mean much. The 1969 Mets were no-hit by Bob Moose four days before clinching their first division title. But it wasn't the most encouraging of vital signs for a lineup whose pulse was erratic at best.

Hints of life would emerge in the days ahead as d'Arnaud returned and the Mets rebounded to take five of six. The one they lost, to Atlanta at Citi on June 13, proved particularly vexing in the moment. On the same day American Pharoah clinched horse racing's Triple Crown at nearby Belmont, call-up Danny Muno (No. 156 in the legendary hot corner procession that dated back to all-time horse player Don Zimmer) spit the defensive bit, committing three errors at third. Yet the Mets galloped to a 3–1 ninth-inning lead. Alas, it was the Braves who put on a finishing kick to land in the winner's circle, via two runs off of Hansel Robles and protective-hatted Alex Torres in the ninth—stallion Jeurys Familia was unavailable to close—and two more off Carlos Torres in the 11th. The Mets happily broke even the day after. They fell behind, 8–2, when Gee couldn't get out of the fourth, but stormed back to win, 10–8. Lagares, d'Arnaud, Dilson Herrera, and rookie outfielder Darrell Ceciliani each homered. All of them were under twenty-six. Was it fair to infer the future encompassed young hitting as well as young pitching?

* * *

The young pitching was so plentiful that Gee's poor outing served as his undoing. With plenty of options for their five- and/or six-man rotation (depending on management's mood), the Mets would designate him for assignment and, once he went unclaimed, leave him at Las Vegas for the rest of 2015. Meanwhile, Syndergaard and Harvey kept firing fastballs and the Mets took two from the Blue Jays in Flushing. Despite the roster fluctuations and the offensive inconsistencies, the Mets had recaptured first place, leading the not necessarily inevitable Nationals by a game-and-a-half as they flew to Toronto to continue their home-and-home Interleague set.

Perhaps it was the currency exchange rate or metric conversion at work, but all at once, the Mets' OPS suddenly essentially added to zero. Over the next seven games in Toronto, Atlanta, and Milwaukee, the Mets scored nine runs. They won none of those games. The fourth of those losses dropped them behind Washington. The seventh loss shoved them under the .500 mark. From a 13–3 start, they had fallen to 36–37. You could point to injuries, inexperience, random chance—it didn't really matter to uneasy Mets fans.

We were rooting for a losing team again and were not immune to assuming it was all downhill from here. It wasn't. The Mets wound up their road trip a .500 team again, scratching out a 2–0 win over the Brewers, deGrom stopping the madness by throwing eight shutout innings and scoring his own insurance run.

In June, it seemed the only way a Met starting pitcher could ensure victory was to do it all himself.

LOCAL BOY MAKES IMPRESSION

In the best tradition of ice cream mogul Tom Carvel, who instilled in a generation of New Yorkers the calendar clarification that "Wednesday is Sundae," Friday was about to become Thorsday. On June 26, Noah Syndergaard made the first of four consecutive Friday night starts. He was as sure a sign of the weekend's arrival as the disc jockeys everywhere who could be counted on to blow the five o'clock whistle and blast Loverboy.

If the 28,109 who eased into Citi Field on this initial Friday-as-Thorsday night had been working for the weekend, it was the Mets and visiting Reds who'd be laboring for runs. Curtis Granderson led off the bottom of the first versus Johnny Cueto with his 12th home run of the season—his fourth to start a game, his 10th with nobody on—and the Reds scratched out a run in the top of the second. From there, Syndergaard and Cueto matched zeroes until the bottom of the fifth. The Mets pushed across the tiebreaker in perfectly 2015 Metsian fashion: a two-out triple from Dilson Herrera; a walk to Granderson; a steal of second by Granderson; a three-two walk to Eric Campbell; and a three-two walk to Lucas Duda.

It was about as reluctant a two-out rally involving a triple as could be stitched together, but the Mets led, 2–1, and Thor made it hold up through eight innings. Jeurys Familia came on in the ninth, threw three ground balls to the heart of the Red order and shoved the Mets above .500 again.

On Saturday, a substance previously in short supply from Montauk to Metuchen and everywhere in between appeared above Flushing: rain. A dry spring gave way to a dry summer, but June 27 proved the unseasonably chilly and ceaselessly wet exception to the rule. I believe the meteorological term for the phenomenon is "lousy day." First pitch was scheduled for 4:10 p.m. First drops were felt seconds later. Why even start, I wondered from my otherwise primo seats in the first row of Excelsior, perfect in every way except for the presence of people somewhere behind me who whined from underneath their protective overhangs that they couldn't see through my portable umbrella. I folded under their harangue and persevered in a poncho.

I assumed the more than 32,000 tickets sold and the relentlessly promoted Steve Miller Band concert that was slated to follow the game influenced the jokers who decided this was a lovely afternoon for baseball. For six innings, it was take the money and rain. The Mets almost got away with it, too. Granderson homered in the third to stake Matt Harvey to a 1–0 lead. The Dark Knight was within two outs of winning a theoretical official game under dark clouds when Brandon Phillips—who has literally never not gotten a hit in any Mets home game in which he has been an opponent—extended his inexplicable Shea/Citi hitting streak to 31 with a fifth-inning RBI double.

Weather forecasting is an inexact science, but it's a certainty that Brandon Phillips is eventually going to do something to a Met pitcher while wearing road grays. The visiting Red machine took the edge off Harvey Day and extended the rainy day longer than it had to go on. After six, with the contest still knotted at one, the umpires finally took mercy on the players and poncho-wearers alike and suspended the action until 1:10 the next day. Even Steve Miller would have to wait until Sunday.

When Sunday rolled around, he and his band would have to wait and wait some more.

* * *

The rain cleared up, but the Mets and Reds wouldn't so easily enter Swingtown. What was still technically Saturday's game kept on rock'n us, baby. The 1–1 affair picked up in the seventh inning and remained 1–1 through 9, then 10, then 11. There would be no resolution until the bottom of the 14th when, with dozens of giveaway life-size Lucas Duda growth charts being waved as talismans, the Mets' slugger put all six feet and four inches of himself into a bases-loaded pitch and produced a mammoth walk-off fielder's choice ground ball to first base. The Reds couldn't convert it into an out at home and the Mets, who left 19 men on base and went a combined 0-for-15 with runners in scoring position, came away 2–1 winners.

It is said they all look line drives in the box score, even if few who populated the Mets box score looked capable of hitting line drives. Nobody who batted in this game carried an average higher than .261. Five Mets were floating well below .200, including three pinch-hitters, a.k.a. players inserted specifically for their ability to hit.

Wins look like wins in the standings however feebly they are wrangled and the Mets now had three straight. They'd go for a sweep of the series in the official Sunday game/ad-hoc nightcap and they'd do it amid what could have passed for a family reunion, for this was the Sunday the Metsies would merge with the Matzes.

That's the Long Island Matzes, a family likely more comfortable with the *Baseball Register* than the *Social Register*.

* * *

The Mets and Long Island were by no means strangers. As early as 1967, sportswriter Leonard Koppett detected that "the Mets had become a deeply rooted Long Island entity," an allusion to geographic proximity, customer base and overall vibe. Four decades later, the region's preeminent contemporary philosopher, Mr. William Joel, declared Shea Stadium was "where New York meets Long Island," and there was no reason to believe the psychic border had shifted more than a few hundred feet east once Citi Field opened. Historically, the Mets were owned by Long Islanders of the upper crust North Shore variety. There were Paysons and deRoulets, Doubledays and Wilpons, Wilpons and Katzes.

Kids of not such affluent means had been growing up on Long Island rooting for the Mets since 1962. In good times and bad (though more, for sure, in good times), Nassau and Suffolk counties constituted the heart of Mets country. Now and then, kids from Long Island who excelled at youth baseball were rewarded with more than a Carvel sundae. These youngsters grew up to be actual Mets. The better-known among them tended to be veterans stopping off after establishing their MLB bona fides elsewhere. Frank Viola of Hempstead, Pete Harnisch from Commack, and Long Beach's own John Lannan all spring to mind in that category. A few signed with the organization and debuted as Mets: Hank Webb came straight outta Copiague; Ray Searage was a Freeport lad; Charlie Williams graduated from Great Neck South. But nobody who was Long Island through-and-through ever made it to the majors as a Met and made it big as a Met.

Steven Matz couldn't have been any more Long Island had he been sitting at an adjacent table in Billy Joel's "Scenes from an Italian Restaurant." The kid (twenty-four, but he looked fourteen) was a product of Stony Brook, a prospect at Ward Melville High School and, perhaps best of all, not just the Mets' second-round draft pick in 2009, but a Mets fan who counted Endy Chavez's sensational catch in the 2006 NLCS as his fondest memory.

Only a true Mets fan would pick a moment that occurred in a loss.

* * *

Steven was a Mets fan before he was a Mets pitcher. His parents were Mets fans. His grandfather, a Brooklyn Dodgers diehard until Dem Bums left him high and dry, was a Mets fan. The Matz bloodlines ran orange and blue. No wonder a party of nearly 150 family members and friends gathered at Citi Field on the last Sunday in June to witness the southpaw's first big league appearance. It probably would have come years sooner had the young man not required Tommy John surgery on his way up the ladder. It might have come in 2015 before June 28 had the Mets not been blessed with a surplus of starting pitchers. It wasn't as if they didn't have enough arms at this juncture of the season. Steven was doing so well at Vegas there was no longer any sense keeping him down on the farm.

The first pitch by a Met pitcher who already had a sandwich named in his honor well in advance of his making the majors came about as close to home plate as the Se-Port Deli in East Setauket—purveyor of the Matz chicken cutlet hero ever since Steven was drafted—sits to Citi Field. For the uninitiated, that's a distance of forty-nine miles. The rookie would find the strike zone soon enough, albeit to his detriment. The fifth pitch Matz threw was belted by Phillips for a home run.

One batter, one run, an ERA of infinity and Matz *mishpucha* everywhere nervously holding their breath. Is this any way to make a local boy feel at home?

Steven took care of the butterflies, then the Reds, surrendering no more than a walk in the rest of the first. He pitched a 1-2-3 second before formally introducing his full complement of baseball abilities as only a National Leaguer could. The Mets were batting in the bottom of the inning, which was unfolding as its usual exercise in non-aggression. Darrell Ceciliani reached on an error and advanced to third on two groundouts. Eighth-place hitter Campbell was walked intentionally to facilitate a likely escape from the slight jam that faced Cincinnati pitcher Josh Smith. Soup entered the game with a .171 average, but why pitch to somebody at least remotely capable of getting a hit when you can just go ahead and face the pitcher?

In the National League, pitchers played on both sides of the ball. Perhaps Reds manager Bryan Price had forgotten. Steven Matz couldn't have. He was a Mets fan. He knew what real baseball looked like. He knew the pitcher hit.

So he hit. Specifically, he doubled, deep to center, driving in both baserunners. Steven Matz of the Mets put Steven Matz and the Mets ahead, 2–1.

That task ably completed, Matz made himself comfortable with his surroundings. Todd Frazier would touch him for a leadoff homer in the fourth, but that would be all the lefty would allow. Steven would single to help build a run in the fifth and, with the bases loaded in the sixth, he'd single again, knocking in a pair of runs. He'd make it deep into the eighth, pitching with a 7–2 lead that the Mets pen secured.

* * *

The Matz family was happy, to say the least, particularly the grandfather, who quickly became known as Grandpa Bert once the SNY cameras captured him exulting like a son of a gun every time his grandson did something wonderful. Mets families from Port Washington to Port Jefferson were thrilled to have discovered yet another live arm let alone a shockingly skilled bat. Matz's four RBIs were the most ever compiled by a pitcher in his major league debut. No Met, regardless of position, had ever driven in more runs in his first game. Steven's ERA was 2.35, his batting average 1.000.

Even Steve Miller took notice. During his band's (sparsely attended) postgame show, he marveled how "Stevie" Matz had reached out and grabbed us, and dedicated "Abracadabra" to his phenomenal debut. The young man's magic was contagious. His catcher, Johnny Monell, conjured the first two-hit game of his career. Campbell, the luckiest eighth-place hitter on the face of the earth, crafted a box score line presumably influenced by the occult: 0 AB, 3 R. Soup had been walked thrice, plunked once, and contentedly accepted three rides around the bases, courtesy of the pitcher who had yet to make an out in a major league game.

The next day, *Newsday* reported the Se-Port Deli was serving an exceptional number of its local-hero heroes, even though it was clearly no longer the only Metropolitan Area establishment where everybody knew Steven Matz's name.

MILD CARD CONTENDERS

As the statistical first half of the schedule wound down, the Mets hadn't shown they could consistently hit, but they were surely hosting with the best of them. With their sweep of Cincinnati put in Howie Rose's books, they could count 29 of their 40 home games as wins, having done exactly what good teams are supposed to do when presented with subpar opposition. Against the Phillies, Marlins, Braves, Brewers and Reds—each of them wallowing below .500 as June edged toward July—the Mets had won 21 of 25 at Citi Field.

Versus quality competition, home *and* away, the Mets needed to step up in class. Either that or arrange some sort of visiting team-in-residence program with the league's lesser lights.

For all their offensive woes, the Mets hadn't fallen off the trail of the Nationals, even if it was generally agreed that Washington was sooner or later going to irretrievably pull away. The Mets didn't necessarily have to concur with the conventional wisdom, but on the off chance that Bryce Harper's MVP-caliber year wasn't going to go for Nat naught, they needed to take their next nine games extremely seriously.

From June 30 to July 8, the Mets were going to be jumping into the National League wild-card race, facing three teams that had their eyes at least partly on this more fraught avenue to the postseason prize. There were the Cubs, who'd be venturing into the unfriendly confines of Citi Field for three; there were the Dodgers, who figured to be less than welcoming to the Mets for three in Los Angeles; and there were the Giants, defending their world championship turf for three more in San Francisco.

If the Mets retained aspirations about catching the Nats, they couldn't afford to lose ground anyway. And if the Nats slipped out of their reach, there was ground to be made up on these conditional wild-card rivals.

* * *

After the off day that followed Steven Matz's rousing debut, six teams jabbed at one another for four playoff spots within a bottom-to-top universe that measured no more than three games tall. The Mets sat a half-game behind the Cubs, who sat a game-and-a-half behind the Giants for the second wild card. The Giants, in turn, hovered a half-game behind the Dodgers, who were in first place in the West—or a half-game from falling back into the wild-card tussle. The Dodgers held virtually the same record as the Nationals, who were in first place by two-and-a-half over the Mets in the East, yet, for what it was worth, a half-game behind the wild-card-leading Pirates.

Only St. Louis, lapping the Central field, seemed a certainty for the postseason. For every other contender in the National League, fluidity ruled.

The wild card, as every baseball-obsessed schoolchild in America knew, was not an ideal destination, as two qualifiers in each league were assigned a one-game death match at the outset of October. But if you emerged from the wild-card battle with your shield rather than on it, then you were a fully vested playoff team with as good a chance of winning the World Series as any division winner. The Giants and Royals proved that the previous fall, ascending to the final round despite the scarlet WC stitched implicitly into their uniforms.

Back when there was just one wild card in each league, the Mets made it their passage to potential glory twice, in 1999 and 2000. They came within two games of the World Series the first time they held the card and earned a pennant the second time. There was nothing dishonorable about getting in via a place lower than first. But it was going to be difficult . . . especially if the Mets continued to use their bats for nothing more than decorative purposes.

In their Citi Field set against the Cubs, there was no evidence that their Louisville Sluggers were anything but props in a movie being shot on location in Flushing. The script involved a baseball team that never, ever scored and probably never would again.

* * *

On June 30, Jon Niese gave up one run in seven innings. The Mets lost, 1–0.

On July 1, Bartolo Colon gave up no runs in seven innings. The Mets lost, 2–0 in 11.

On July 2, the Mets scored a run. It could have been mistaken for an urban legend, but it really showed up on the scoreboard. In the third inning, with one out, Jacob deGrom doubled. With two out, Curtis Granderson doubled. The Mets really and truly scored a run. Hallelujah!

* * *

Sadly, deGrom had the nerve to give up several and the Mets lost to Jake Arrieta, 6–1. They were once more a .500 ballclub, 40–40. In numerical terms, they were not good and they were not bad. They simply were.

Was this any way to contend for the wild card? Probably not. The Cubs had surged into that second spot, a game-and-a-half up on the Giants and three-and-half over the Mets. The Nationals had picked up a game on the Mets as well during the wrong-way sweep. If the Mets could be had at home, their commitments on the road loomed as even more treacherous. Away from Citi Field, the Mets did not resemble contenders. At 11–26, they looked more like the teams they'd so easily beat up on at home. The next two games, three thousand miles away, would bring them into contact with practically perennial Cy Young Award winner Clayton Kershaw and lately untouchable Zack Greinke. Greinke hadn't given up a run in any of his previous three starts and he was going to face a team that tallied exactly one in its last three games.

Daniel Murphy had returned during the Cub series, but Travis d'Arnaud was out again, having sustained an elbow injury in a home plate collision on the last trip to Atlanta. David Wright would be with the Mets in LA, but only for a stop 'n' chat; he was rehabilitating his back in Southern California and there were no baseball activities in his immediate future. Terry Collins was going to have to keep making do with his collection of Eric Campbells, John Mayberrys, and Johnny Monells. In another year, that would've been par for the course. This year felt different in April but was teetering on the brink of sickening familiarity in July. Midseason West Coast swings were where faint Met hopes traditionally went to wither en route to expiring.

HOW WE GOT
GOING AGAIN

WESTERN SWING

California wasn't the place you'd instinctively pick for the Mets to get their season back in gear. Then again, California wasn't the place you'd pick for the Dodgers and Giants to be calling home if you were watching them at Ebbets Field and the Polo Grounds in the decades prior to 1958. You never know where you'll begin to find your answers in baseball. For the 2015 Mets, Chavez Ravine was as reasonable a spot as any to start rediscovering themselves.

The Mets did little against Clayton Kershaw on July 3 at Dodger Stadium, which is not the same as saying they did nothing. A little was enormous, considering the caliber of the pitcher and the offense's recent sample size. Down 1–0 in the fourth, John Mayberry led off with a double, moved to third on a wild pitch and, one out later, scored on Wilmer Flores's single to right. The run put Friday's child Noah Syndergaard on an even footing with Kershaw and Thor made the most of it, going six, striking out six and allowing only two hits to first-place Los Angeles.

Kershaw tamed the Mets through seven, leaving it for the bullpens to figure out. In the top of the ninth, Dodger closer Kenley Jansen permitted a bloop double to Lucas Duda, couldn't handle a liner back to him from Flores and then gave up a sacrifice fly to Kevin Plawecki to make it 2–1, Mets. It wasn't much of a rally, but after Jeurys Familia turned away the Dodgers in order, it represented the winning run and gave the Mets a winning record as they closed out the first half of their schedule at 41–40.

The 2015 Mets were four games better than they had been at the halfway point of 2014, although they had never been remotely involved in a race a year earlier. Progress was undeniably being made. I mean, come on, they had just beaten Clayton Kershaw. Could they beat Zack Greinke, too?

No, unfortunately. Progress wasn't being made that fast.

* * *

Greinke extended his scoreless streak to 27 2/3 innings and lowered his ERA to 1.48 by blanking the Mets over seven on the Fourth of July. Matt Harvey was going to have to be close to perfect to match him this Saturday night. He wasn't. Harvey struggled with command—seven hits and five walks in five innings—and left trailing, 3–0. The Mets stirred late against the Dodger pen, but lost, 4–3.

With the Nationals beating the Giants that same afternoon, the Mets fell four-and-a-half out of first, their largest deficit of the season. That was the bad news. The good news was the Dodgers hadn't yet developed the technology to clone Kershaw and Greinke. On Sunday, LA was out of aces, while New York's just kept coming.

Steven Matz's second major league start suggested he didn't need to pitch in front of family and friends to succeed. Across six innings, Matz allowed only two hits and two walks while striking out eight. Freed from facing the Cy Youngnoscenti, the Mets grabbed an early lead on Dodger starter Mike Bolsinger, added to it and then fortified it against his successors. The Mets took the rubber game, 8–0, with Matz having to drive in only one run this Sunday. Perhaps Steven was good luck all around. The Mets had scored 15 runs in his two starts, yet were held to six in the five games in between.

The Matz-luck link would suffer a blow soon, however, as the rookie was about to be diagnosed with a partially torn lat muscle (when you're a Mets fan, you sure learn a lot about the human anatomy). He wouldn't pitch in the majors again until September. Lest it seem the Mets only had pitchers go *on* lists that might keep them from participating in their first playoff chase in seven years, one name popped *off* the ineligible list after the Mets arrived in San Francisco.

Jenrry Mejia, who had been suspended in April for testing PED-positive, was back on the roster. Visions of a lockdown bullpen danced in the head of any Mets fan who noticed what Kansas City did the previous

October with Kelvin Herrera, Wade Davis, and Greg Holland. Bobby Parnell, the closer of record from 2013, had already returned from his lengthy Tommy John rehab and wasn't giving up runs as he acclimated to a setup role. Give Parnell the eighth. Give the presumably clean and easily forgiven Mejia, who had nailed down all those saves in 2014, the seventh. Jeurys Familia, who had done almost nothing wrong in the first half of 2015, could continue to handle the ninth.

It would be The Closer and The Closer and The Closer—sort of like, I decided, the 1978 *Saturday Night Live* sketch in which Walter Matthau, as adviser to Dan Aykroyd's Richard Nixon, dreams up a ticket sure to get his politically disgraced client restored to the Oval Office in 1980. Nixon would run once more for president, with former president Gerald Ford as his veep. Matthau's slogan:

The President and the President
For President and Vice President

* * *

It's a long season. My mind tends to wander.

While Terry Collins and pitching coach Dan Warthen calculated where Mejia fit in the bullpen line of succession, the Matz-less offense resumed its nap. Against the Giants on Monday night, July 6, Chris Heston gave up three hits more to the Mets than he did in New York nearly a month earlier, but just as many runs. No-Hit Heston had to settle for taking a shutout into the eighth and having nothing to show for it . . . which was business as usual for Jon Niese. Niese went eight, scattered three hits of his own, allowed no runs and exited for the evening. The Mets and Giants proceeded to the ninth in scoreless fashion.

Due up for the Mets were a handful of players voted most unlikely to break a tie.

* * *

Leading off, Michael Cuddyer, playing first base less to get his bat in the lineup than to keep Duda's out of it. Cuddyer's average had sunk to .236. His body of work from June 20 through July 5 consisted of 36 at-bats and two base hits.

Next, Kirk Nieuwenhuis, quietly designated for assignment/oblivion in May and briefly alighting in Anaheim before the Angels decided they didn't want him anywhere near Los Angeles, at least not on their dime. The Angels waived Kirk and the Mets waved him back into their organization, perhaps out of habit. They stashed him in Las Vegas before recalling him at the outset of the San Francisco series. He started the night batting .100 as a major leaguer in 2015, .079 as an April and May Met.

Third, Johnny Monell, fourth-string catcher, give or take an Anthony Recker. Johnny had recently gotten hot and pumped his average all the way up to .182.

These were the men who the Mets were depending on to break a 0–0 tie.

* * *

Y'know what, though? Nothing ventured, nothing gained. Cuddyer lashed a single to left off Sergio Romo. And Nieuwenhuis—after failing to bunt him over—doubled to right, sending Cuddyer and his balky knee to third. And Monell, facing Giant closer Santiago Casilla, doubled. The Mets led, 2–0, on the fourth and fifth RBIs of Johnny's major league career (his last ribbies of the season) and held on to win, 3–0. It was a team effort personified.

The same team dropped a 3–0 decision the next night, but the July 8 finale provided a San Francisco treat. Jacob deGrom, the only All-Star chosen from the relatively resurgent Mets, outlasted Jake Peavy and stymied the defending champs. Just two hits and one walk in eight innings, with ten K's thrown in for emphasis. It was an All-Star performance adequately supported for a 4–1 Met win. A notable addition to the Mets arsenal was the long ball. Eric Campbell's ninth-inning homer, a two-run shot off Jean Machi, was the Mets' first dinger since two Saturdays and 10 games earlier, that day in the rain against the Reds when Curtis Granderson went deep.

A power bat at last. Power arms throughout. The power of a positive thinking to match a road trip whose results landed on the happy side of .500. The Mets went 4–2 in California, taking consecutive series from a pair of teams answering to the same description as them: contenders. With one series remaining before the All-Star break, it was a reminder that being in a race could be powerful stuff.

THREE METS & A BREAK

Numerologists who favored "3" had to love the Mets in mid-July. In their final series before the All-Star break, at home against the Diamondbacks, the Mets swept three games.

On July 10, Noah Syndergaard made his third consecutive Friday night start and the Mets won for the third Friday in a row. On this Friday, the 13 strikeouts to emanate from the right arm of Thor were the most breathtaking element in a 4–2 victory.

On July 11, Matt Harvey was one of three Mets to homer, marking the third consecutive game in which the Mets went deep. On getaway day in San Francisco, they had the one from Soup Campbell. The night before, the long balls were produced by Lucas Duda and Michael Cuddyer. On Saturday afternoon, Harvey was joined by Duda and Ruben Tejada en route to another 4–2 win. It was the third consecutive game in which the Mets prevailed by scoring four runs.

On July 12, Kirk Nieuwenhuis hit three home runs all by himself. Considering Nieuwenhuis was a .106 hitter entering Sunday's action and that he hadn't hit a home run all year, this development rated as somewhat more shocking than Harvey's two-run shot the day before, let alone Thor's 13 K's Friday. What made it flat-out historic is that no Mets home game in their fifty-four-year history had ever been graced by a three-home run performance by a home player. It had never happened in the Polo Grounds, it hadn't taken place at Shea Stadium, and Citi Field had never seen anything like it until now.

Kirk Nieuwenhuis: historic Met (and .143 batter at day's end). Daniel Murphy chipped in one home run himself to help Jon Niese earn a 5–3 victory, keeping going not just the team's winning streak but the pattern of increasing the Mets' daily power output by one. After nine consecutive games with no home runs, the Mets had slugged 10 in their previous four.

* * *

There was another three that rated attention as the Mets completed their sweep of the Diamondbacks. Jeurys Familia saved each game against Arizona, plus that last one at AT&T Park, raising his season total to 27, or one fewer than Jenrry Mejia had saved during the entirety of 2014. Familia was more dependable than Shea's old Armitron clock. You could set your watch (or smartphone) by him.

It can be debated whether saves are the best metric by which to measure a closer's worth, but watch a few ninth-inning leads evaporate and it's incredible how important they seem when you don't get them. Familia was getting them on the most regular basis imaginable. Jeurys had blown all of two saves to date in 2015 and both were games the Mets came back to win. He'd absorbed no losses, he'd let only one of 13 inherited runners score and his ERA was a scant 1.25.

Due respect to every Met closer from John Franco to Mejia, this was an upgrade over what were used to. What we were used to was overwhelming tension and throwing things in our living rooms. The sabermetric acronym measuring the emotional scars inflicted at the worst possible instances over the past quarter-century was probably OMG (or Armand-OMG). Familia all but eliminated the psychic pain. A lead of three or fewer runs in the ninth inning was no longer something to view as tenuous. Jeurys was arguably the Mets' first-half MVP.

Yet he wasn't a Mets All-Star. The honor that had been bestowed on Franco (1990), Armando Benitez (2003), Billy Wagner (2007 and '08), and Francisco Rodriguez (2009) eluded the closer who made us breathe easier than any of those talented if angst-inducing fellows ever had. Familia was squeezed by the system that required a representative from every team and—as we learned the year Armando was pity-shoved onto the squad—when a team doesn't have a legitimate All-Star, their closer tends to get the call.

Hence, Jonathan Papelbon, with 14 saves for the 29–62 Philadelphia Phillies, was a 2015 National League All-Star, while Jeurys Familia, with 28 saves for the 47–42 New York Mets, was not. Clearly, personality was not the deciding factor.

So although the Mets were five games above .500 and only two games out of first place at the break, they were limited to one All-Star.

But what an All-Star.

* * *

The Mets' man in Cincinnati on July 14 was the richly deserving Jacob deGrom, who had followed up his Rookie of the Year campaign with half a season worthy of whatever award is given to sophomores. The inadequacy of won-lost records to reflect a pitcher's performance was illustrated in deGrom's 2015 thus far. He was a 9–6 pitcher on paper but the guy you could count on when you weren't certain about anything else. Syndergaard was getting better all the time, but he was still learning. Harvey may have been the Dark Knight, but even a superhero has his ups and down in his first year back from an injury. Niese never didn't make a person nervous and Bartolo Colon, both ageless and a wonder, couldn't help but sometimes remind you of his mileage.

DeGrom you expected to come through every fifth or sixth or whatever day he came up in rotation. And he usually did. His ERA was 2.14 at the break. He had given up more than three earned runs only twice in 17 starts. His specialty seemed to be final games of series the Mets absolutely had to have: eight one-hit, shutout innings against the Cardinals in May; another eight scoreless versus the Brewers in June; the eight in which he blanked the Giants in July. Plus, DH be damned, he was hitting .205.

They weren't going to let pitchers bat in the All-Star Game, but Bruce Bochy knew enough to send deGrom to the mound in the top of the sixth inning at Great American Ball Park. The lone officially sanctioned stellar Met faced three American Leaguers.

He struck out three American Leaguers.

Down went Stephen Vogt, swinging. Down went Jason Kipnis, swinging. Down went Jose Iglesias, swinging. Except for a stray ball to Kipnis, deGrom was flawless. None of his three batters made any contact whatsoever. In 10 pitches, nothing whatsoever was hit, not even foul. It was the kind of All-Star performance that made a Mets fan proud all out of proportion to what the moment signified in the standings. Jacob now stood with Ron Hunt starting the 1964 All-Star Game at Shea, Lee Mazzilli stealing the show at the Kingdome in 1979, and Doc Gooden making all of baseball sit up and take notice at Candlestick in 1984. Every generation needs a Midsummer Classic Met memory of its own. This one had the kid with the long, flowing hair and the side he retired with verve and panache.

After Nieuwenhuis's homers, Familia's saves, and deGrom's strikeouts "three" may have been the numerological theme of the week, but there were, foremost, two undeniable takeaways from the All-Star game:

1) The National League lost despite deGrom's mastery and thereby ceded home field advantage in the World Series.
2) A Met pitcher showed himself to be untouchable on the national stage.

Both were items that might come in handy to know a few months down the road.

A MARATHON, NOT A SPRINT

The first two games the Mets played after the All-Star break, at St. Louis, they lost. One was a 3–2 heartbreaker, one was a 12–2 blowout. The third game is probably still going on in some distant precinct of the universe.

Here on Earth, the Sunday, July 19 series-ender at Busch Stadium did eventually come to a conclusion, though in real time it couldn't have felt more endless or more futile or more perfect a distillation of how difficult it was for the Mets to generate the offense necessary to contend for a playoff spot.

It was also a decent advertisement for how the Mets never quite gave up no matter the difficulties they encountered.

If you've ever wanted to be sentenced to spend eternity inside the Draft Kings commercial that ran every half-inning on SNY for six months— next to those bros at the bar forever awaiting daily fantasy resolution and riches—this was the game for you. Across 18 innings and nearly six hours, the Mets and Cardinals wouldn't stop doing nothing.

* * *

The Mets and marathons are grudging old acquaintances that can't stay away from each other for long. The flagship of the franchise's extra-inning line continues to be their very first voyage into the great beyond, the 23-inning, 7:23 doubleheader nightcap against the Giants at Shea on May 31, 1964, won by San Francisco and umpired by Ed Sudol. The

Mets would play two games with more innings to them (24 in 1968, 25 in 1974, with Sudol somehow calling balls and strikes in both) and stay up much later to complete another legendarily lengthy contest (the 3:55 a.m., 19-inning, Rick Camp-homering, fireworks-exploding, 16–13 Fulton County affair of 1985), but the 1964 edition endures foremost among the enduring.

It was the second game of a doubleheader that lasted 32 innings. It was the game that came within a half-hour of reaching a new month. It featured a triple play, Willie Mays at shortstop, and Ed Kranepool playing all day and all night after playing a doubleheader the day before in Syracuse for Triple-A Buffalo. Whenever the Mets give their loyalists an excuse, they will talk about this game.

My favorite aspect of May 31, 1964 (received second-hand, as I had just turned seventeen months old and can't say I remember tuning in), is the story of John Daly, host of CBS's *What's My Line?* introducing his broadcast that Sunday night with the honest admission that he'd been backstage watching the most "marvelous"—or in one retelling "fantastic"—baseball game between the New York Mets and San Francisco Giants just before coming on the air that evening. Why, it had been going on for hours and was still going on well past regulation, here at 10:30 p.m. on the East Coast.

Panelist Dorothy Kilgallen fretted that John must stop expressing his fascination at once, for if he extolled its virtues any further, he would risk chasing Metropolitan Area viewers from their show on Channel 2 to that very game on Channel 9! Legend has it that countless dials clicked seven notches up the VHF spectrum to see what exactly at Shea Stadium had Daly so riled up, and there went the rating for that night's *What's My Line?*

* * *

In our splintered media universe of more than a half-century later, I wondered if anybody anywhere who wasn't already watching our Metsies go on and on opted to set aside whatever popular culture he or she was consuming in order to sample a taste of extra, extra innings 2015 Mets-style. If so enticed, did they find it marvelous? Was it fantastic?

If you were new to baseball and tuned in to decipher the fuss inherent in a ceaseless 0–0 game, I can't imagine it necessarily sold you on the virtues of the National Pastime. And if you are a hardened fan of several decades, chances are you were tempted to weep—or maybe just sigh a lot—for the farce your beloved game had become. Still, no matter why you found yourself watching the Mets and Cardinals from Busch Stadium on that Sunday afternoon deep into Sunday evening, I can't imagine you could've pulled yourself away.

That is the appeal of a marathon game wedged in the midst of a season that we are continually taught is a marathon and not a sprint. No matter how poorly it is executed (and no matter how much you believe its participants *should* be executed, or at least designated for assignment), it keeps going. Even if you maintain a strict rooting interest, you are torn between wanting the definitive run scored by your team and desiring no such thing because then it will be over. You may have things to do, places to go, people to see, but never mind all of those concerns. You are ensconced in what is becoming one of the longest baseball games you will ever experience.

Deep down, you don't want it to end. You want to see where this thing goes and if it can go any further beyond that.

If you were a willing prisoner of your own morbid curiosity, the Mets and Cards were cooperating with your wishes. They weren't going anywhere for the bulk of six hours and neither were you. Certainly Mets batters weren't going any further than third base, for that was the signature of this particular marathon dance between ancient rivals. This one wasn't about spectacular fielding or dazzling strategy or mano-a-mano slugging. It was only sort of about clutch pitching; the pitching was effective as far as it went, but it was difficult to ascertain whether the pitching was smothering the hitting or the hitting was absolutely useless.

There were plenty of hits logged before it was over, actually: 16 from the Mets, 13 from the Cardinals. We had learned on Saturday night in St. Loo that Met hits don't necessarily lead to runs. The Mets accumulated a dozen hits in the game before this one but scored only twice. The Mets of midseason were expert practitioners in the art of making copious amounts of noise without creating a discernible sound, except for the sound of silence. If you attached a microphone to home plate in hopes of hearing the bottom of a spike cross it, you wouldn't hear a peep.

We knew how the Mets could be, and to a degree this was simply a display of their adherence to a philosophy of passive resistance. What was the Cardinals' excuse? Weren't they the best team in baseball with the best opposition research, as evidenced by their alleged hit and run on the Astros' computer system? Shouldn't they have hacked into the Mets' mainframe for at least one run when the Mets were depositing and abandoning everybody from Wilmer Flores (stranded after a one-out double in the second) to Kirk Nieuwenhuis (stranded after a one-out double in the 12th)?

* * *

Credit Jon Niese, he who regularly pitched without support or particular joie de vivre, for the first seven-and-two-thirds of scoreless ball. It was a grim task, but there is no one more suited for sucking the action out of a baseball game played under unyielding clouds. Niese was grimly great for as long as Terry Collins would allow him to be. It wasn't until the eighth, when he hit the newest Met-killer, Randal Grichuk, that he was removed to make way for his fellow veteran, Bobby Parnell. Like Niese, Parnell had been a stoic Met since Shea Stadium stood. Unlike Niese, the bushily bearded Parnell hadn't shaved since Citi Field opened.

No situation was too hairy for Parnell. He struck out the dangerous Jhonny Peralta— all Cardinals are dangerous—and it was off to the torpid races from there. The Mets had a chance to go ahead in the ninth, if you interpret a baserunner as synonymous with a chance. Eric Campbell walked with one out. He was still on first with two out when he decided stealing was the better part of valor. Kevin Siegrist picked him off and was in the dugout enjoying a cool beverage before Soup was tagged out at second.

And on they went. The Met relief corps—Parnell in the ninth; Jenrry Mejia for the next two, Hansel Robles during the inning after that—kept the Cardinals at bay. The Cardinals seemed determined to disavow their Runnin' Redbirds reputation and jogged as slowly as possible on most of their own batted balls. Everybody had an excuse. Yadier Molina was tired from squatting. Matt Holliday was recovering from an injury. Carlos Villanueva was a pitcher. Even the Best Fans in Baseball booed impatiently when Villanueva didn't take advantage of a potential infield flub in the 12th . . . and much of the crowd that remained by then was sticking around for the sharing of postgame Christian Day testimony with special (and extraordinarily patient) guest Kurt Warner.

* * *

Thou shalt not pass on scoring opportunities was the key commandment of a game schlepping into the 13th. The Mets, at last, heard The Word, because they jumped on the energy-conserving Villanueva pronto. Curtis Granderson, who hadn't started in deference to lefty Tim Cooney pitching for St. Louis, lashed a leadoff single that he deemed worthy of stretching into something more. Curtis sped up and was safe at second. While Keith Hernandez was in the booth audibly moaning for "a whiskey—please," Granderson helped himself and made his own double.

Kevin Plawecki was up next and found the first significant hole of the day, not counting the 24 holes in all those doughnuts on the scoreboard. Kevin's grounder darted between Kolten Wong at second and Mark Reynolds at first. Granderson, who had earlier attempted to inject life into listlessness with an unlikely stolen base, kept running as the rest of Missouri sleepwalked. He scored an actual run. The Mets had an actual lead.

The Mets liked the sensation so much, they tried to extend it. Ruben Tejada singled Plawecki to third. A sacrifice fly would make it 2–0, so on the off chance that the next Met pitcher gave up a leadoff home run, the Mets would still be out in front. Though Campbell tried his best to make a worthwhile out, his fly to right was too short to send Plawecki home. Juan Lagares, in one of his 10 at-bats, made one of his eight outs, also not long enough to aid the greater cause. Daniel Murphy was intentionally walked, bringing up Robles's spot. Collins looked down his bench, shrugged and called for Johnny Monell.

Monell popped up. The Mets didn't tack on an insurance run. Disappointing, but not unexpected. Prior to Plawecki's hit, the Mets were 0-for-Ever with runners in scoring position or, really, any position. Still, a 1–0 lead was better than a perpetual 0–0 tie, and besides, Jeurys Familia, the All-Star in terms of everything but being named one, was coming into pitch. Familia had saved the last four wins the Mets had compiled. He couldn't have been any better rested, not having worked in a week. All he had to do was . . .

You didn't have to be a game-show whiz to know the answer. Familia gave up a leadoff home run to Wong in the bottom of the 13th. He had to. A 13-inning, 1–0 win would have been relatively simple. On the other hand, a 13-inning, 2–1 loss would have been brutally painful. Familia played his role in the marathon perfectly. He put two more runners on before striking out Tommy Pham to guarantee a 14th inning.

* * *

There are exceptions to every rule, but extra-inning games don't start running toward marathon status until they reach the 14th. Keith could sigh and moan and ache for the sanctity of the sport he held dear every eight seconds, but until we knew we had a 14th inning—by which the time the LOB had been declared the official state bird of Flushing—we couldn't be sure we were experiencing something we'd be referencing way down the road. Like the 23-inning game from 1964. Or the 24-inning game from 1968. Or the 25-inning game from 1974. Or the 19-inning game from 1985 that ended with fireworks at four in the morning. Or the 20-inning game at this very ballpark in 2010, one that also nibbled at the edges of sanity with its offensive ineptitude, except Fox did that one, so we couldn't sit inside Keith Hernandez's head and watch it ooze out of his ears.

SNY was blessedly on the air this Sunday and Keith's entertaining disdain was running wild in the streets of downtown St. Louis. Thank heaven for small favors.

Now that Collins and Mike Matheny were legitimately low on personnel, a technically dull game was promising to get incredibly interesting. Matheny would eventually turn to starter Carlos Martinez. Terry went with perpetual mystery guest Sean Gilmartin, a pitcher whose identity would surely stump Dorothy Kilgallen, Arlene Francis, and Bennett Cerf. Gilmartin, in case you'd forgotten, was the pitcher who was kept on standby because he was obtained in the Rule 5 draft. Rule 5 specifies that you must keep Sean Gilmartin on your roster all year long. Rule 6 presumably dictates that you keep forgetting Sean Gilmartin's on your roster.

Gilmartin pitched very well for someone who barely existed. He took care of the Cards with ease in the 14th and 15th and worked out of a bit of a jam in the 16th. Martinez, who came on in the 15th, had the easier job. He had to face the Mets, the pennant contenders who'd left 18 runners on base thus far on top of the 11 from the night before, all while scoring a grand total of three runs in 23 innings.

That's a lot of zeroes to get to a 1–1 tie, but it takes a lot of nothing to go a long way when you're running a Metsian marathon. Martinez was no less successful than his seven pitching predecessors. A double play erased a hint of an uprising in the 15th; a single to Gilmartin (!) and a walk to Lucas Duda (a.k.a. Lucas Nada or Lucas Do Nothing; I hadn't decided) led to three meek outs in the 16th; the theatrical loading of the bases in the 17th, featuring an intentional walk to Murphy to set up an unintentional walk to pinch-hitter Jacob deGrom (!!), merely served to adorn Lucas's two-out strikeout.

The Mets walked 13 times and not one base on balls led directly to a run. The Cardinals literally couldn't give this game away.

Carlos Torres, whom I tended to refer to as Carlos Tsuris when he wrought *mishegas* on the mound, did the Mets a mitzvah by not bringing the Mets trouble when he replaced Gilmartin in the 17th. Tsuris, make that Torres, struck out his first two batters, surrendered a base hit, but then benefited from Plawecki gunning down Peralta on an attempted steal of second. Molina may be the bee's knees of catchers over the last decade, but Yadier was outshone in this particular marathon by young Kevin.

Perhaps had Aaron Heilman pitched, Molina would have had a greater impact on the outcome.

* * *

At last, a different chapter unfolded from all those that had preceded it. The 18th inning brought a sustained Met offensive onslaught. Flores singled. Granderson singled. Plawecki bunted and confounded Martinez. The bases were loaded again, with absolutely nobody out. The National League would be legally compelled to fold operations if the Mets couldn't push one lousy run across.

Two were forthcoming, one via Tejada sacrifice fly, one via Campbell suicide squeeze. The latter couldn't stand as an isolated moment of triumph, however, as good ol' Soup got himself thrown out at first upon further review mostly because he slowed down en route to glance over his shoulder at the play at the plate. It was terrible baseball instincts, but perfectly understandable from a human standpoint. If you were clinging to a spot on the sub-.200 Met bench of 2015, maybe you were well off eschewing the best advice of Satchel Paige. Sure, go ahead, look back—something probably *was* gaining on you.

With a third run in and a franchise record-tying 25th runner left on base (yes, the Mets had done this before, in the '74 all-nighter), all that could go wrong instead went uneventfully right. Torres set down what was left of the Cardinals in order and the Mets had themselves a 3–1 win that took 18 innings, ran five hours and fifty-five minutes and, with the notable exception of Keith Hernandez's will to live, rendered no casualties. The Christian Day pilgrims, like the nocturnal fireworks enthusiasts of Atlanta, indeed stayed inside the park to hear old Rams QB Warner share his "incredible story," which certainly had a new coda to it after that long an afternoon and early evening.

The entire Christian Day package was billed in advance by the St. Louis sales office as "a wonderful day of faith and baseball." Considering Sunday's particulars and how it all worked out from our perspective—frustration, followed by aggravation, followed by deliverance, followed by a flight to Washington to take on an alleged powerhouse first-place club still only two games ahead of ours in the standings—I wouldn't say there wasn't truth in *that* advertising.

THE SCHEME OF THINGS

In the scheme of things, a second-half series pitting the first-place club versus the second-place club when the two clubs are separated by two games looks pretty substantial. There's no arguing the Mets saw their upcoming three-game set at Nationals Park as a major stepping-stone in their season. Terry Collins had set his rotation to have his three aces ready. How often since 2008 had the Mets played three games against anybody after the All-Star break with any kind of implications for their own fortunes? The Mets-Nats series loomed as the Mets' biggest in seven years.

Nevertheless, it wasn't going to solve the puzzle for 2015 all by itself. The Mets would have 67 games remaining when the series in DC was over, the Nats, 69. Save for a psychologically damaging sweep by the home team, the Mets figured to emerge alive no matter what.

* * *

The Monday night game on July 20 didn't get the proceedings off to the desired start. Matt Harvey was down, 5–0, after three, and despite his righting himself to last seven (and driving in two in the fourth to temporarily salvage his own cause), the Mets came out on the short end of a 7–2 score.

In case anybody needed reminding, Tuesday made clear why Jacob deGrom was an All-Star: six innings, eight strikeouts, three baserunners. Unfortunately two of them were clustered in the fifth, and the second of them was a Wilson Ramos home run, leaving deGrom on the wrong end of 2–1. Jacob was removed for pinch-hitter Eric Campbell in the seventh with two on and one out, even though Jake was batting .195 and Soup was down to .174. The move worked anyway, as Campbell plated both runners to let deGrom leave as the pitcher of record on the winning side. The Closer and the Closer and the Closer—Mejia, Parnell, and Familia—finished up what became a 7–2 result in the Mets' favor.

The bullpen blueprint got smudged the next day. Noah Syndergaard handed a 3–1 sixth-inning lead off to Hansel Robles, who passed it along to Mejia in the seventh. So far, so good. But come the eighth, Parnell gave out, allowing three National runs. Drew Storen came on in the top of ninth, struck out the side, and preserved a 4–3 Washington win.

The Mets would leave town three games out of first place. It felt like more, but the standings don't require stand for emotional interpretation. Three out with 67 to play was not bad . . . not bad at all.

* * *

But this offense? For 95 games, with a few exceptions, it had been ragingly inadequate. In the 96th game, it would at last prove internally unacceptable. The Mets were back in New York on Thursday night, July 23, starting a four-game series against the West-leading Dodgers. Clayton Kershaw was again their opponent. This time they couldn't remotely touch him. That in itself is no shame or crime. Kershaw was the reigning Cy Young and MVP. He was about to commence a characteristically dominant stretch drive.

It was the way the Mets went about not touching him. This was the lineup Collins sent out to face perhaps baseball's best pitcher:

Granderson, .251
Tejada, .255
Flores, .248
Mayberry, .170
Campbell, .179
Duda, .236
Lagares, .256

Recker, .137
Colon, .147

Even allowing for the manager avoiding lefties against the lefty Kershaw and sitting Murphy . . . even understanding that Colon generally pitched better when Recker caught . . . even remembering that Mayberry doubled against Kershaw in LA three weeks earlier . . . even taking into account the injuries that had ravaged the Mets' depth since April . . . even granting that batting averages aren't the be-all and end-all of hitting metrics . . . even with all of that in mind . . .

. . . this was not a lineup capable of taking on somebody who had won three Cy Youngs. This lineup wasn't capable of going up against Anthony Young while he was losing 27 straight decisions. Unsurprisingly, Kershaw threatened to retire 27 straight batters. He had a perfect game going through six and left with a three-hit shutout after eight. Colon had given up only one run through the same eight innings, but one run was a bridge too far for these Mets to cross. Two ninth-inning runs off Sean Gilmartin and Carlos Torres ensured a 3–0 Met defeat.

At Pittsburgh, the Nationals lost, too, keeping the Mets three games on their tail. If it weren't for Nat lethargy and Met pitching, this wouldn't be much of a race. We could applaud the out-of-town scoreboard all we liked, yet if the Mets remained incapable of putting runs on their own board, Washington wouldn't have to do much to win the division by default. The wild-card derby was getting dicier and dicier, but again, it didn't matter what the Pirates, Cubs, and/or Giants did if the Mets were going to do nothing at the plate. A summer of swinging and missing was going to continue if the Mets were going to do nothing in the front office.

Something was about to be done. The scheme of things was about to be dramatically altered.

HOW WE GOT
TRANSFORMED

NEW FACES OF 2015

When the season started so promisingly, Steve Kettmann appeared to be a prophet. Kettmann was the author of a book called *Baseball Maverick*, a study of Sandy Alderson—part biography, part organizational analysis. Whatever the book's strengths (and there were several), the element that drew the attention of the Mets-obsessed was its subtitle, wherein the general manager was credited with having "revolutionized baseball and revived the Mets."

What was prophetic in April verged on laughable in late July. To paraphrase from Alderson's baseball writers' dinner quip of a couple of winters earlier, "What revival?" Never mind that the book was published when the Mets were coming off a 79–83 finish. Never mind, even, that the Mets were barely keeping their heads above .500 as August approached. While the Met offense sank further and further into the abyss, Alderson had revived nothing more than a sense of doom.

You say you want a revolution? All we wanted was a couple of decent guys off the bench.

* * *

The trading deadline was July 31, but the limit of Mets fan patience was reached eight days earlier with the infamous Mayberry-batting-cleanup, Campbell-batting-fifth game against Clayton Kershaw. While both John and Eric seemed like fine gents and certainly possessed baseball skills most of us watching in the stands or from home couldn't possibly dream of having, they were not what you'd call the heart of a lineup.

Enough already, Maverick. It was time to revive the roster.

The first step came July 24 in the form of a nice, round number and an improbably inexperienced name. The Mets called up, from Double-A Binghamton, left fielder Michael Conforto, their No. 1 draft pick from 2014, to be a) part of the solution and b) the thousandth Met ever. Conforto's status as Mr. 1,000 was a coincidence, but his ascent to the bigs definitely seemed like a milestone. Alderson's regime had been working the draft since 2011. Their first three top picks—Brandon Nimmo, Gavin Cecchini and Dominic Smith, high school kids all—were talented but nowhere in sight for 2015. Conforto, on the other hand, was a college star who pushed himself onto the immediate radar by excelling at St. Lucie and then Binghamton. Plus, there was no better option. Less than 700 at-bats into his professional career, Michael was a Met.

His career picked the same night to be born as Tatum Jeffery Niese, son of Jonathon Joseph Niese, which would make for an adorable footnote, except Niese the elder decided to pitch as scheduled versus the Dodgers that Friday night, which was both admirable and probably a little foolish, considering Jon had every reason to be distracted. L.A. lit Niese's celebratory cigars but good, as the Dodgers defeated the Mets, 7–2. Conforto christened his Metsness with an RBI on a groundout.

* * *

The novelty of the One Thousandth Met didn't last long, because Alderson moved to bring in Messrs. 1,001 and 1,002, dealing with the self-decimating Braves for exactly the kind of utilitymen for whom the Met reserves were crying out louder than Tatum Niese. Coming to the Mets for a pair of minor league pitchers were Kelly Johnson and Juan Uribe. Each had played on playoff teams. Uribe could model a World Series ring on each hand if he so chose, one from the White Sox in 2005, another from the Giants in 2010. If you subscribed to the Every Five Years rule, Uribe was—à la Leah Niese on Friday—due.

So were the Mets for the kind of night that unfolded during their newest acquisitions' first game on Saturday, July 25. More than 39,000 fans were in attendance at Citi Field, partly for the postgame performance by Heart, partly to see how much heart the reinforced Mets might show.

They had heart. And hits: 21. Almost every Met in the starting lineup was a magic man. Conforto went 4-for-4. So did Kirk Nieuwenhuis, who drove in four runs. Daniel Murphy knocked in three, Matt Harvey two. Lucas Duda homered twice, while Johnson welcomed himself to Flushing's good graces by going yard. The Mets went full barracuda on the Dodgers and devoured a victory, 15–2.

* * *

The tenor of the festivities would change the next afternoon. Sunday was a day for pitching, as Jacob deGrom faced off against Zack Greinke. Greinke entered the game in the same untouchable state the Mets had found him three weeks earlier, his scoreless-innings streak having reached 43 2/3. It would extend by two more innings, but the third marked its undoing. Greinke hit Nieuwenhuis to lead off the inning, then allowed a single to Kevin Plawecki. An error by center fielder Joc Pederson put Kirk on third, from whence he dashed home on deGrom's grounder to first. Nieuwenhuis beat Adrian Gonzalez's throw and Greinke's streak was over at 45 2/3.

Jacob cradled the 1–0 advantage like it was the Nieses' newborn. How often does a pitcher hold a lead against Zack Greinke? The Mets gave him another run in the sixth—Conforto taking his first MLB HBP with the bases loaded—as the Dodgers looked helpless. Jacob crafted his own score-less streak, seven and two-thirds innings of shutout ball, on two hits, two walks and eight strikeouts. The Mets' All-Star prevailed in this classic pitchers' duel.

But he wasn't so easily awarded a win. Jeurys Familia bailed Jacob out of slight trouble in the eighth, but the ninth showed even a mostly dominant closer could be had. Two consecutive doubles—the second by former Met turned current nemesis Justin Turner—halved the 2–0 lead and a single tied it up. After not scoring in the ninth, the Mets were headed to extras.

Jenrry Mejia came on to make 36,000 or so Mets fans a little nervous when he walked Jimmy Rollins and couldn't stop him from stealing second or advancing to third on a sacrifice. Jenrry calmed everybody down in short order, though, striking out Pederson and flying out Howie Kendrick. When Curtis Granderson led off the bottom of the 10th with a double and came around when new hero Uribe banged a hit off the left-center field wall, Mejia secured the 3–2 victory and his first win of the year.

Also, his last.

* * *

This scintillating Sunday was the last we'd see of Jenrry Mejia in 2015. By Tuesday, news would come down of a second suspension for the reliever. It was PEDs again, and this time he was pronounced gone for a year. As it happened, another Alderson acquisition was already in the books. During Monday's off day, the Mets made another trade, obtaining Tyler Clippard from the Athletics. The timing seemed convenient, but the GM said he'd had no inside dope (so to speak) that Mejia was about to be suspended. Either way, given Familia's mini-slump, a little bullpen aid figured to be an enormous help as July neared its end and the next weekend's series with the Nationals, this one at home, loomed on the horizon.

First though, the revamped Mets had some business with the Padres, a three-game set that began encouragingly enough on Tuesday the 28th, with Noah Syndergaard (8 IP, 9 SO) and Clippard shutting down San Diego, 4–0. Washington lost at Miami, putting the Mets a single game out of first at 52–48. New York had played exactly 100 games and, when you considered all they'd been through, couldn't have been in much better shape.

After what they'd go through in the next forty-eight hours, you'd be excused for thinking they'd never recover.

HUH?

It is an article of faith that if you go to a baseball game, you'll likely see something you've never seen before. After the two baseball games I attended on July 29 and 30, I can attest to that.

The Mets lost to the Padres, 7–3, on Wednesday night the 29th. Something like that I've seen plenty. Bartolo Colon had One of Those Starts and the Mets were never really in it. I've seen good pitchers throw bad games. Lucas Duda launched three home runs, which I'll admit I'd never seen before—and no Mets fan had seen a Met do at home before, unless he or she was at Citi Field earlier in the month when Kirk Nieuwenhuis did the same thing in a win. Duda's feat was impressive, but by the time it was completed, it what wasn't what causing a buzz on the 7 Super Express to Woodside.

Something nobody had witnessed before did happen. It didn't show up in the box score. Well, the player at the focus of the unprecedented incident did show up in the box score, which is what made it so unprecedented. Or so we thought.

* * *

The date of the game is consequential in establishing the singularity of what happened. July 29 was two days from July 31. Sandy Alderson wasn't done trying to improve the Mets. You didn't need a BBWAA card to know that. The trading deadline loomed. For all the upgrades around the edges, the Mets still needed one more player, one more piece. They needed someone who could be projected to make a serious impact on the pennant race.

Because we all bring our smartphones to the ballpark, and I'm as guilty as anybody of checking mine when I should be watching Colon pitch or Duda swing, I was as wired into the trade rumor mill as everybody else. I had Twitter.

Therefore, I knew something that wasn't posted on the scoreboard or announced over the public address system. I was privy to a scoop (me and thousands of other obsessives). I knew the Mets had made a huge trade. They were getting Carlos Gomez.

Carlos Gomez! Former Met prospect. Made an impression as a rookie in 2007. Went to Minnesota as part of the bounty for Johan Santana. Eventually blossomed into an All-Star for Milwaukee. Blazing speed. Surprising power. Flair and charisma. A true impact player fending off injuries this year, but just what we needed!

We were getting Gomez in exchange for Zack Wheeler, whose name had been barely uttered since March, and Wilmer Flores, who didn't yet hit enough to justify his tentative fielding. Flores was the starting shortstop more by default than out of conviction. Yes, Wilmer's power potential was alluring, but he hadn't homered since June 12 and he did little for proponents of strength up the middle. The Flores-Murphy DP combo demanded breath-holding on every ground ball. Maybe we'd regret the eventual development of a slugging shortstop who wasn't quite twenty-four, but as with trading Gomez to get Santana in 2008, this wasn't about the future. This was about now.

Now we knew Gomez would be the piece. Now we knew Flores was going. Now we saw Flores in the game we were watching and . . .

* * *

Huh? Why is Flores still in the game? Don't they usually take guys who are about to be officially traded out of games so nothing queers the deal? The vast majority of beat writers, columnists, and insiders were tweeting this deal was done. Gomez was a Met. Wheeler and Flores were Brewers. Wilmer being on the field trying to help what was about to be his old team beat the Padres was strange, but maybe an undotted 'i' or uncrossed 't' was floating about. Perhaps it was no longer protocol to remove your nearly traded players from active competition. It wasn't like this happened every day, so who knew how this was supposed to work?

Some of us did, at least where our part was concerned. My friend Ben and I didn't need to consult the Basic Agreement to understand our role in this story. We may not have necessarily loved Flores more than any other Met, but we liked him well enough. He seemed like a nice kid. He tried hard to make himself an adequate shortstop. He'd been one of ours.

So when his next at-bat came, even if he was all but technically a Brewer, we stood and applauded. Good luck, Wilmer, we were saying in the seventh inning. We were not alone (though the entire stadium was not on its feet—it was a sultry evening and not everybody was clued in to the breaking news). It was a simple fan gesture, not a lot different from the salute we gave Bobby Abreu on Closing Day 2014. Bon voyage and all that . . . now when's Gomez getting here?

Flores took his at-bat, grounded out, innocently elicited some more applause and then mysteriously trotted back to short for the top of the eighth. Surely Wilmer Flores, Milwaukee Brewer, had participated in his final Met moment in that last plate appearance. Surely Collins had been instructed to pat him on the fanny and point him to the traveling secretary.

* * *

Surely something was awry. It was back to Twitter to learn tears were in Wilmer Flores's eyes. Ben and I were in right field Excelsior, so we couldn't see his face, but the folks watching at home got a very good look. I unraveled a pair of earbuds and turned on the transistor radio I keep with me for those moments when I need Howie Rose and Josh Lewin to explain the inexplicable to me. They were watching their monitors and reported, yes, our shortstop was crying. Our section had access to monitors, too. I turned to my left, looked up, and saw close-up after close-up of young Wilmer Flores.

He looked liked he'd been told to leave the only organization he'd ever known.

Who among us thinks of stuff like that when we're celebrating an net upgrade to our team's roster? Who remembers that Wilmer Flores signed with the Mets out of Venezuela when he was sixteen? When I was sixteen, I was watching Lee Mazzilli win an All-Star Game for the National League. When Wilmer was sixteen, he was a professional baseball player employed by the New York Mets. It was eight years later. Wilmer had been a Met—minor and major leaguer— for a third of his life.

While it was being processed that this was excruciating for one of the players involved, it still defied reason that Wilmer Flores continued to play shortstop in this very game. He'd obviously learned he was being traded. What was wrong with Terry Collins?

Nothing, it turned out, except for Collins being one of the few people at a baseball game who doesn't stare at his phone between pitches. The manager had no idea until the murmurs overtook the ballpark that Wilmer Flores was being traded. Alderson hadn't told him because— get this— Wilmer Flores wasn't being traded.

Huh again?

* * *

There is a distinction between "being traded" and traded. "Being" indicates an action taking place. Alderson and his Milwaukee counterpart, Doug Melvin, were working on a deal and were finalizing the details, but it didn't come to pass. Twitter was a good place to divine this, too, but not before we were all mentally dressing ourselves in spanking new Gomez wear. In the prehistoric past when reporters had only themselves and their editors with whom to ponder rumors, none of this would have leaked out into the world. You might hear later that a trade almost happened, but something that didn't happen wouldn't make the paper. Papers didn't come out every nanosecond. Twitter does. Twitter's part of the baseball landscape, particularly as July 31 approaches and everybody needs to know ASAP what's going on.

Nothing went on. After the game, an agitated Alderson said there was no trade (his and Melvin's version diverged on what nixed it—Gomez's health or Gomez's contract). A simmering Collins was at a loss to understand these Wi-Fi times. Why, he wanted to know, were people looking at their phones during a ballgame anyway? It seemed a disingenuous protest, given how many *"take out your mobile device!"* come-ons pierce Citi Field's mid-inning pauses, but Terry wasn't hired to moderate a New Media roundtable; he was trying to win with the players he had at his disposal. Last he checked, Flores was one of those players. When Wilmer's spot in the batting order came around again in the ninth, Collins pinch-hit for Wilmer, but by then, the image of July 29 as the night the Mets didn't know what they were doing was seared into the baseball consciousness.

The #LOLMets hashtag caught fire. Collins wouldn't have known it was meant to imply laughing out loud at the Mets was the default response to everything the franchise did.

Oh, and the Nationals won. The Mets were two back. But at least they'd have the opportunity to shake it off the very next afternoon, in a 12:10 start against the Padres, a Camp Day special. And who would argue by now that the Mets weren't reaching new heights and/or depths of camp?

* * *

The club sat Flores on Thursday the 30th and hoped to move on. Personally I hoped they'd dwell on what just happened, maybe have some fun with it. After all, July 30 would have been Casey Stengel's 125th birthday. The Ol' Perfesser took 120 losses and turned them into lemonade when he was just a lad of seventy-two. Casey's Original Mets weren't merely traded in tweets. They were, as the punchline goes in Harry Chiti's case, traded for themselves.

When I returned to the steamy ballpark on Thursday morning, this is what I would have loved to had greet me:

- Flores merchandise (if there was any) on closeout special in the team stores, but just for one inning. Attribute the sudden sale to an unavoidable misunderstanding.
- The splicing of 2007 Gomez highlights into the usual rally reels to see if anybody noticed.
- The retirement of Wilmer's No. 4 in a touching pregame ceremony . . . and then the unretirement of it in a slightly less touching pregame ceremony five minutes later.
- A PSA in which Collins urges all fans to use their mobile devices with utmost caution— "or better yet, just watch the game while you're at the game."
- Wilmer's endorsement of GroundLink Transportation, the official ground transportation provider of the New York Mets: "I may not know

whether I'm coming or going, but I can always depend on GroundLink to get me somewhere."

- A montage of Wilmer's home runs (assuming they were adaptable to modern technology; it felt like he hadn't hit one since kinescopes) set to a loop of Gary Cohen's "OUTTA HERE!" calls. And then bring the soundtrack to a screeching halt.
- Wheeler as the answer to every trivia question, since it seemed we'd all kind of forgotten who he was.

The Met powers that be, killjoys that they are, didn't take me up on any of my suggestions (which I had helpfully tweeted). What they were doing on the field was perfectly fine, however. They built a 7–1 lead behind Jon Niese and appeared poised to take the rubber game of the series and send the camp kids and big kids alike home reasonably sated.

Except, as we learned the night before, appearances surrounding the Mets can be deceiving.

The Padres made up a big chunk of their deficit on one swing, when Derek Norris lifted a grand slam off Hansel Robles in the seventh (after Bobby Parnell loaded the bases). The Mets' lead was down to 7–5, but no worries. Tyler Clippard pitched a scoreless eighth and Jeurys Familia was ready for the ninth.

So were storm clouds. Literal storm clouds. The blackest, thickest storm clouds you'll ever see, accompanied by thunder that grew louder by the moment. The storm was coming. Three outs were needed. Familia would be advised to get them quickly. The Promenade, where I sat with my buddy Joe, was not built to withstand the clearly impending meteorological Armageddon.

I weighed the benefit of remaining in my seat for a theoretical final out versus leaving myself open for end times if I didn't take shelter soon. Seriously, those clouds were dark.

The next clap of thunder emanated from, I estimated, directly above the Mr. Softee stand in the food court a few sections to our left. It was a little too close for comfort, especially considering how little comfort had been available to us all day. A six-run Mets lead had been recently whittled to two; I was drenched in enough sweat that you'd have thought I'd just hustled over from opening for Bette Midler at the Continental Baths; and

Camp Day was still going surprisingly strong and surprisingly loud. Since before noon, Camp Day kids had been responding to every Noise Meter tickler the Citi Vision board had put before them, as if they needed the challenge. Their screams weren't as loud as the thunder, but they were unnerving in their own way. These children were still screaming nearly three hours after they'd begun.

Put it all together, and it was enough to drive a diehard toward a life preserver.

* * *

"I'll meet you after the last out," I told Joe, hoping "last out" wasn't to be taken literally, as in the last out prior to the impending rapture. I excused myself and left Joe and his scorebook to fend for themselves, positioning myself to watch the last outs . . . maybe the last outs ever . . . from the concourse.

Familia made swift work of the first two Padres, as the rain began to fall. Baseball games with only an instant or two left to them could withstand a shower, even a downpour. The Dodgers eliminated the Phillies from the NLCS in that kind of rain in 1977. The Giants did the same to the Cardinals in 2012. This was just the Mets and the San Diego Padres in the heat of nothing more than a summer's day. Surely they could dance another couple of steps between the raindrops and give Joe and me and the campers something to enjoy on our respective ways home . . . assuming we weren't all being Called Home in a different vein.

There would be no next instant for Familia, no next pitch for more than half-an-hour. The weather started getting rough; Citi Field was tossed; if not for the courage of the Mets grounds crew, the infield would be lost.

The next thunderclap was more like a standing ovation, and not for a shortstop who thought he'd been traded. This one said *Get out of the stands, get off of the field, get out of the monsoon that is about swallow Flushing whole.* I was met down in the concourse by Joe and by everybody else. Hundreds of campers remained and now needed to be corralled by counselors who probably didn't sign up for this particular duty. Every boom of thunder and every crack of lightning was met with shrieks you hadn't heard since Luis Castillo circled under a pop fly one borough away.

The counselors tried to distract their campers by leading them in rep-
etitious chants, somehow skipping Let's Go Mets. At their and our feet,
lagoons like you'd see at Shea Stadium . . . lagoons the size of Shea Stadium . . . formed. To call them puddles is to refer to the Atlantic Ocean as
your bathtub. The rain blew in horizontally. Security shooed the curious
from sticking as much as a head out from under for a clearer look at the
thick, gray skies. They could not be held responsible for your imminent
extinction if you did.

The video screens showed *1986 Mets: A Year to Remember,* as if to give
us one final pleasant memory before we were washed away for good.

* * *

The rains subsided, then evaporated. The camp groups were able to
depart. Citi Field grew quiet, save for Larry Keith's expert narration and
the Duran Duran soundtrack that emphasized just what wild boys Lenny
Dykstra and Wally Backman were back in the day. Dozens remained along
the first base side of Promenade, Joe and I among them. The seats were too
wet to sit in, but that wasn't a big deal. We weren't going to be long.

At 3:15, when we'd been standing around for about twenty minutes,
it was announced the two teams would retake the field at 3:30. One more
out would be recorded and we could all go home. The grounds crew was
diligently sweeping away the water that sat in front of the Padres dugout,
which I thought was a lot of trouble to go to for just one out's worth of
baseball. This was a Pine Tar Game conclusion for the 21st century, a lot
of trouble being gone to for the sake of the record books, because it certainly wasn't for the fans. There was hardly anybody at Yankee Stadium
that makeup night in 1983 and few of us were hanging in here at Citi Field
in 2015.

Around 3:25 the field looked fairly immaculate. We were antsy to
see the end of our 7–5 Mets win. Did they really have to wait until 3:30?
Couldn't Norris get his ass up to the plate now? Couldn't Terry send in . . .

Hey, who was Terry going to send in? Familia looked fine getting those
first two outs, but we were staring at something like a thirty-five-minute
delay. Jeurys was going at it in the Flushing tropics and then he was sent,
I'm guessing, to cool his heels in an air conditioned room. Aren't pitchers

supposed to not be left to their own devices for that long a period? Wasn't Carlos Torres fresh and capable of a single out with nobody on?

Familia returned to the mound. Oh well, I tried to rationalize, Terry might actually know his pitchers better than I do. Maybe the rain delay won't have an effect on Jeurys. "Water and rain have always been a blessing to me," Pedro Martinez wrote in his memoir, referring to the 2005 night Shea's sprinklers surprised him in the midst of pitching. "That's what this felt like." Perhaps it would feel the same for Familia.

* * *

Six minutes later, all blessings had turned cursed. As we stood behind an unoccupied Promenade Box section, Norris the devil Friar stayed alive on an 0-2 count before dropping a hit into short right field; he was now 5-for-5. Matt Kemp poked a fast grounder through a hole just to the right of Ruben Tejada, who was playing short while Flores took his mental health day. Next up was Justin Upton, who lined Familia's second pitch far and deep to center, through the raindrops—for they were falling anew—and over the fence.

Over the preceding weekend, Padres television announcer Dick Enberg was in Cooperstown accepting the Ford C. Frick Award for excellence in baseball broadcasting. Enberg showed off his Hall of Fame chops when, as Upton circled the bases and gave San Diego an 8–7 lead, he suggested, "It's not just the rain that's falling at Citi Field. How about the hearts of Mets fans?"

Yes, how about our hearts, to say nothing of our heads, which Upton's swing had conveniently banged against the outfield fence for us? Justin was probably just trying to be helpful, knowing how good it feels when one stops banging one's head against a wall. Except Mets fans of the highest order don't know how to stop.

Rain-loving Pedro Martinez, who had also been upstate a few days earlier to accept his induction into the Hall of Fame, took a moment in his speech to identify with those of us who cheered him on between 2005 and 2008. "The Mets fans," he said, "well, if you look at me and you see me going wild, that's a Mets fan. That's how we are. So Queens, I love you, too!"

I gotta tell ya, Joe and I were going wild in rainy Queens, but not with love. As soon as Jeurys captured the elusive and somewhat irrelevant third out of the top of the ninth, Joe—as peaceful a sort as you'd be fortunate to know—punched the hell out of an abandoned craft beer cart. He must have released a secret spigot, for the rain intensified. The bottom of the ninth, the Mets down by one, would have to wait.

The wind kicked up again. The grounds crew attempted to unroll the tarp. The tarp attempted to roll up the grounds crew. The game was on pause yet again.

We weren't. We decided to stop with the heads and the walls and the banging, at least for however long it was going to take to play again. The Mets could lose, 8–7, without us on hand for the predictable denouement. As it happened, we had time to catch the local to Woodside, change for the LIRR, change at Jamaica and be in our respective homes and still not miss a thing. The second rain delay lasted close to three hours. The bottom of the ninth lasted about thirty seconds. Craig Kimbrel retired the Mets in order, sealing the first Mets' home loss after leading by six runs since 1970.

* * *

That year was my first full season as a Mets fan. I got hooked during the stretch run in 1969, but 1970 was the year I saw how baseball really worked. I saw that you don't get a miracle every year. I saw the Mets come up vary-ing degrees of short for sixteen consecutive seasons until 1986. And then I saw 1986, like 1969, was not something easily repeated.

Like every Mets fan old enough, I'd been watching since 1986 without the benefit of ultimate reward. Every Mets fan too young to have 1986 as a year to remember had been watching without knowing personally and fully how great being a Mets fan could be. Together, our lives seemed to often boil down to twenty-four-hour periods like this one: trades not made and leads not held.

Yes, Mr. Enberg, our hearts did fall, but they had an Amazin' resilience built into them. Save for the occasional ungodly deluge, we weren't going anywhere. You heard Pedro. That's how we are.

SOMEONE FOR THE
REST OF US

Before the rains ruined Camp Day, the out-of-town scoreboard flashed the news that the Nationals won again, 1–0, on a combined three-hitter from Max Scherzer, Drew Storen, and their new closer, Jonathan Papelbon. The erstwhile Phillies All-Star seemed a curious pickup, but the Nationals felt he fortified their bullpen and that there was no reason their former closer Storen couldn't flourish in a setup role. If there was any good to come out of Washington's win, it was that the Mets wouldn't have to see Scherzer, who Matt Williams didn't bother to save for the weekend series at Citi Field, the first critical, if not crucial, series in Citi Field history.

Terry Collins set his rotation as he had for the recent series at Nationals Park: Matt Harvey on Friday, Jacob deGrom on Saturday, Noah Syndergaard on Sunday. But the Mets still had some fortification of their own to take care of. Even in the aftermath of all that went wrong against the Padres, they were only three out and the calendar suggested time remained to pull a win out *before* first pitch Friday night. It was still July 30, still Casey Stengel's birthday, still time left to shop for that one gift that might make all the difference or at least help the Mets close the gap on the Nats.

* * *

We knew Carlos Gomez was off the table. Milwaukee wound up sending him to Houston. We assumed Harry Chiti (dead at the present time, in

Stengelese) was probably not available, either. As July 30 became July 31 and the 4:00 p.m. trading deadline loomed, Sandy Alderson and his lieutenants kept working the phones. Everybody who followed these things, professionally or otherwise, remained wired into the situation, the undone deal of Flores and Wheeler for Gomez be damned. It was another day for Twitter, another day to dine on rumors.

The Mets were maybe going to get Justin Upton, the same guy who did them in on Thursday. Nah, that wasn't going to happen.

The Mets were maybe going to get Jay Bruce from the Reds. The Mets could use his power. Zack Wheeler might be enough to make this happen. It hadn't been so long ago that Wheeler was the trading deadline apple of the Mets' eye, the prime pitching prospect of the defending world champion San Francisco Giants in 2011. The Giants were interested in what was then "now" and gave him up for Carlos Beltran. Beltran did not lead the Giants to another title (it wasn't his fault; the Giants only win in even-numbered years). The Mets wanted future in 2011—Wheeler, twenty-one at the time, would someday team with Harvey in a rotation that would bring the Mets back to prominence.

It wasn't working out quite that way. The Mets were in a race, but Wheeler was nowhere near it. His elbow injury sent him back to the future, so to speak. The Mets needed help in 2015's now. Wheeler wouldn't be of any use until 2016 . . . except as a trade chip. They liked Wheeler, but they really needed offense. Bruce had 17 homers.

Wilmer Flores could show how much he didn't want to be traded by being moved to tears. Zack Wheeler couldn't be quite so spontaneously dramatic, so he took a moment from post-Tommy John rehab to call Alderson.

Don't trade me was his message. *I want to stay a Met.* Unlike Flores, it wasn't as if he'd never been in another organization. Like Flores, he was quite fond of the organization he was in. What a revelation it was to learn some players felt as loyal to the Mets as the fans did.

Alderson didn't necessarily pull out of Wheeler-for-Bruce because of Zack's request, but he did admit hearing it had an impact on his thinking. Besides, as four o'clock grew closer and closer, he had another deal cooking.

* * *

The Tigers, drifting from contention, were in seller mode. One of the contracts they wanted to get something for was Yoenis Cespedes's. Cespedes was a familiar figure in Citi Field lore. He won the 2013 Home Run Derby when the All-Star Game came to Flushing. Cespedes hit balls to parts of the park that Mets fans had never seen reached by their own sluggers. The Cuban defector had been the subject of a bidding war when he came to the US a few years earlier. The Mets weren't up for anteing then. But this was now. Cespedes, who generally played left, was owed only two months' salary.

He could run. He could hit. He could hit for power. He could field. He could throw. Since when did the Mets get a guy like this, even as a rental? As the rumors thickened Friday like the clouds had Thursday, the Mets fan mindset focused on just one name. Never mind Gomez. Never mind Upton. Never mind Bruce.

Give us Yoenis Cespedes.

* * *

Alderson did. With mere minutes remaining before the deadline, it was confirmed. The Mets were sending two minor league pitchers—one of them righty Michael Fulmer, a legitimate prospect—to Detroit. The Tigers were getting somebody maybe we'd regret giving up down the road. We were getting Cespedes in return, a real, honest-to-goodness star-type ballplayer right here, right now.

Fulmer could grow up to be the reincarnation of Dizzy Trout, Denny McLain, and Jack Morris rolled into one for Detroit. That wouldn't matter if Yoenis Cespedes was a reasonable facsimile of Donn Clendenon, the slugger who made the Mets batting order a genuine threat after arriving at the 1969 trading deadline. It was worth a shot regardless of the outcome. Young pitching we had. Serious slugging we lacked.

We were so set for starters that Wheeler's absence was never felt. Once Kelly Johnson and Juan Uribe alighted, we had a bench. Familia's foible from Thursday notwithstanding, we seemed to have a fairly decent bullpen with Tyler Clippard on board. We were about to have our catcher Travis d'Arnaud return from injury. We had the potential of Michael Conforto, who kept finding a way to avoid demotion. We had Curtis Granderson, who had steadied, and Lucas Duda, who was heating up of late. And now we had Yoenis Cespedes, who rhymed with Festivus, but instead of taking a Seinfeldian holiday to air our grievances, we were prepared to sing the praises of what these Mets were poised to become.

The Mets, who seemed so absurd Wednesday and Thursday, appeared markedly improved headed into Friday's series opener against the Nationals. #LOLMets? Why, yes, you did have to Like Our Lineup.

Mets fans bring the noise to Citi Field for the 2015 home opener.

On the first Harvey Day in nearly twenty months, Matt pitched as if he'd never been gone.

Juan Lagares reaches out and grabs a fly ball as the Mets latch onto an epic winning streak.

Jerry Blevins got the most out of his left arm until it left the stage early in the season.

Travis d'Arnaud goes down the same day as Blevins, and the little hurts begin to create a big void.

Thor what it's worth, Noah Syndergaard takes his much anticipated place in the Mets' rotation.

Long Island pride heads west, as Steven Matz and his relatives descend on Queens.

Extended absences meant accelerated debuts. Kevin Plawecki (22) became one of several rookies to make an unscheduled impression.

Meet Mr. 1,000: Michael Conforto's call-up represented a franchise milestone, not to mention a shot in the offensive arm.

Kirk Nieuwenhuis to the third power: an unlikely candidate becomes the first Met to slug three homers in his home park.

Jacob deGrom shines at the All-Star Game in Cincinnati.

Wilmer Flores had reason to be glum. He thought he was no longer a Met.

Wilmer Flores had reason to be thrilled. He knew he was a Met hero.

Where once John Mayberry and Eric Campbell struggled, Yoenis Cespedes and Lucas Duda went deep.

Midseason cavalry arrived in the form of Kelly Johnson and Juan Uribe, each riding in from Atlanta to provide desperately needed depth.

Yoenis at Coors, getting the best of the Rockies.

A healthy lineup, including d'Arnaud, put the Mets squarely in the swing of things.

Bartolo Colon might flip a ball anywhere, even behind his back.

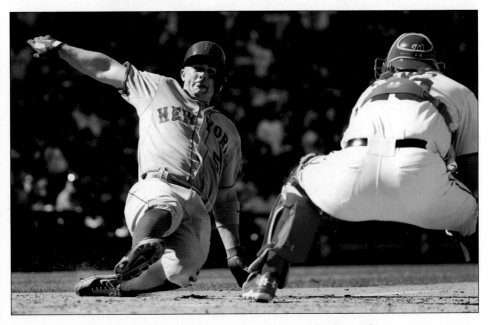

The Captain comes home with a vengeance, spinal stenosis be damned.

A last out for first place: d'Arnaud and Jeurys Familia
clinch a division title.

Curtis Granderson, 2015 Met stalwart.

A September celebration.

Sandy Alderson and Terry Collins turned 79–83 into 90–72 and then some.

Chase Utley misses second base altogether, while Ruben Tejada bears the brunt of a villainous takeout slide.

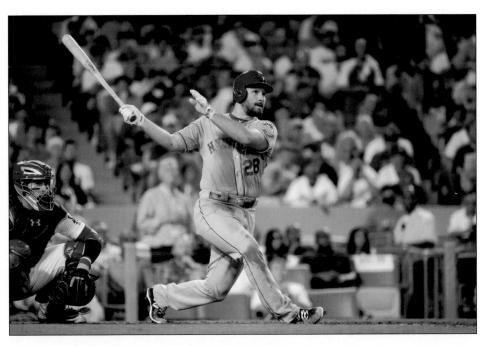

The Greatest Show on Murph unfolds in Los Angeles.

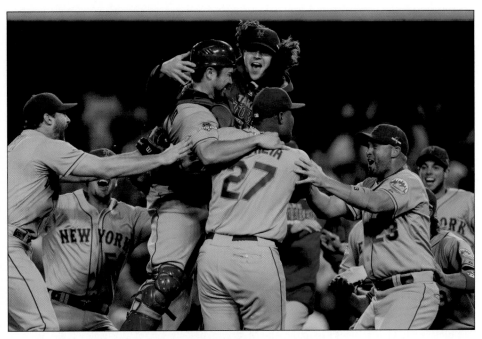

The Mets seemed pretty happy throughout October.

Daniel Murphy defined an unforgettable postseason.

No matter what the movies predicted, the Mets clinched a pennant at Wrigley Field on October 21, 2015.

Collins edges to within spritzing distance of Mets loyalists in Chicago.

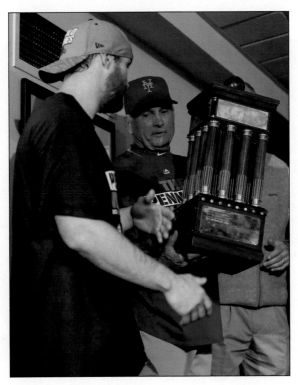

Murphy, Collins, and the spoils of National League victory.

The World Series returns to the Mets' doorstep.

Billy Joel, the Royals, the Mets, and all of New York were in a Fall Classic state of mind.

HOW WE GOT ROLLING

ONCE IN A BLUE MOON

As of July 31, Yoenis Cespedes was a Met. He was not at Citi Field yet, though. The trade with Detroit was completed too late in the afternoon to whisk him from Baltimore, where he'd been spending his last moments as a Tiger, to New York by 7:10 p.m. for the opener against the Nationals, but his presence was felt. To the 36,000 coming through the ballpark gates, knowing Cespedes would be on hand Saturday was a bigger deal than Free Shirt Friday.

Also as of July 31, Wilmer Flores was still a Met. Given how he almost wasn't on July 29, the Generalissimo Francisco Franco treatment was probably in order. He was almost traded on Wednesday, held out of action on Thursday, but back in the lineup on Friday. Some combination of appreciation for the Met who wanted to be a Met so bad he wept when comprehending he might be something else and the intoxication we felt for having just gotten Cespedes turned the shirt-receivers their own kind of emotional. When they got a load of Flores in his first at-bat since the trade that wasn't, they rose and applauded.

Thank you, Wilmer. Thank you for being here. Thank you for being you.

This sort of gratitude isn't readily associated with the Mets fan species, but standing ovations now followed Wilmer Flores around like a loyal pup. He couldn't step into the batter's box or approach a ground ball without his every movement causing a commendatory commotion. Driving Juan Uribe home with the first run of the night in the fourth made him only more beloved.

* * *

Things were going the Mets' way. Cespedes . . . Flores . . . Matt Harvey. Hey, remember him? Matt retired the first fifteen Nationals he faced. That was a perfect game. Lack of Washington baserunners or not, this was a perfect game in so many respects. Big stakes, big crowd, an extra-large charge pulsating through the stands. A playoff race might fit Citi Field better than those free shirts allegedly fit all.

If it felt like this sort of thing happened only once in a blue moon, maybe it was because this sort of thing was happening under a blue moon. July 31's night sky featured the second full moon of the month, which is how astronomically minded folks define the term. None had ever hung over Citi Field while the Mets were in action there. This was the first time there'd been a blue moon in three years, the last time there'd be a blue moon for three more years.

Mets fans recognize the phenomenon not from anything they picked up watching Neil deGrasse Tyson, but because of trades not made, trades that got made and Nationals who make outs. Once in a blue moon, tinged with generous shades of orange, the cosmos could seem unnaturally kind to our fortunes.

The Mets continued to lead the Nationals, who had somehow never gotten around to leading the Mets by as many as five games, by one run. What the heck was their problem? They were the prohibitive favorites to run and hide in the East from the moment they signed Max Scherzer. Bryce Harper, too haughty to settle for a free shirt any day of the week, stoked the hot stove league fires when he asked rhetorically, "Where's my ring?" He was expressing his excitement that Scherzer was joining a staff already anchored by Stephen Strasburg and Jordan Zimmermann, but the offhand remark came to symbolize a sense of National entitlement.

Where were their rings? Where was their runaway? While we were waiting for David Wright to heal, the Nationals were dealing with their own injury problems. Anthony Rendon missed the first two months of the season. Jayson Werth went down in the middle of May and had only just come back. Denard Span had been out since early July. Given how much talent the Nationals packed, it was reasonable to assume they could compensate, but after winning two division titles in three years, they never got fully untracked. Harper was in the midst of the MVP season that had been predicted for him since birth (OPS entering July 31: 1.153), but otherwise, Matt Williams had thus far led Washington to little more than a tenuous divisional edge and a sense that things weren't going as well as they were supposed to be.

But at least they weren't going to be perfect-gamed or even no-hit. Jose Lobaton singled to break up that fantasy in the sixth, but Harvey kept the shutout alive into the eighth. Unfortunately, by the time the Nationals finally eked out a run, the Mets' bats had resumed their pre-Cespedes nap. Harvey, as was his wont, had to leave with a hellaciously well-pitched no-decision: 7 2/3 IP, 5 H, 1 BB, 9 SO, and just the one run.

* * *

Tyler Clippard, former National, finished out the eighth for Harvey. When he ran into a bit of control trouble in the ninth, Jeurys Familia came on and showed no ill effects from the rain-of-terror on Thursday. He got the last two outs of the ninth and, when the Mets couldn't score in the bottom of the inning, all three outs in the tenth in order. Familia was succeeded to the mound by Hansel Robles and Carlos Torres in the 11th and 12th, and each of them was perfect. The Mets pen faced fifteen Nats batters, gave up two walks (both Clippard's) and no hits. The Nats' pen was solid from the fifth through the 11th as well. For the 12th, though Drew Storen and Jonathan Papelbon were in uniform, Williams stuck with rookie Felipe Rivero to pitch a second inning.

It was a short one.

Rivero's first batter was Flores. Flores saw three pitches. The last of them was seen flying over the left-center field wall and onto the Party City Deck.

"Wilmer Flores Night at Citi Field comes to a fitting close!" Gary Cohen enthused over SNY, indicating the hearts of Mets fans were inexorably on the rise.

Under a blue moon, the party at Citi Field was on. It had taken the better part of seven seasons to commence. The perennially new ballpark, forever in search of a defining moment signaling spiritual transformation, had never seen anything like it.

* * *

A walk-off home run.

A walk-off home run that was struck on the night that ended the day the Mets made their biggest in-season trade in years.

A walk-off home run that was struck by the player who shed tears at the thought of being traded two days before and was now embraced from head to toe from one end of Citi Field to the other.

A walk-off home run that was struck in the heat of a battle for first place, a position the Mets had just risen to within two games of by dint of the 2–1 final.

A walk-off home run that was underscored when Wilmer Flores, in the instant that he prepared to step on home plate and into the group hug of his hippity-hoppity teammates, grabbed emphatically at the M-E-T-S on his chest, perhaps expressing his conviction that he was wearing the best shirt of all this Friday.

* * *

After a conclusion like that, was there any doubt the Mets would sweep the Nationals and move into a virtual tie for first place? Logically, of course there was doubt. The other team was still plenty potent and the Mets were on no more than a one-game winning streak.

But c'mon. Were the Orioles going to come back on the Mets in Game Five after Agee and Swoboda did their respective things in Games Three and Four? Did the Red Sox stand a chance in Game Seven after Bill Buckner made Game Six a household phrase?

Could you believe 1969 and 1986 were filtering into our thoughts? What Flores wrought was straight outta comparisons to the most sacred of Met miracles. You're not kidding around when you start invoking the championship years.

But the 2015 Mets weren't kidding around anymore, either.

* * *

On Saturday night, in front of nearly 43,000, Cespedes arrived—and didn't Matt Williams know it. The Nationals nicked Jacob deGrom for two first-inning runs, but the All-Star righty hung tough and gave up nothing else through six. Joe Ross's shutout bid ended with two out in the fourth when Lucas Duda took him deep to bring the Mets within one. In the bottom of the seventh, Duda dinged Ross again, on the very first pitch to knot the game at two.

Two homers for Duda. You'd avoid pitching to a guy on a tear like that, wouldn't you?

Williams wouldn't. And he could prove it.

Curtis Granderson led off the home eighth with a double. With one out, Cespedes was presented with his first RBI opportunity as a Met. The man was brought to Queens to drive in the baserunners too many Mets to date hadn't. Nothing doing, Williams decided. He wasn't going to let the Mets' new big bat beat him.

So he let the Mets' old big bat do it.

Duda—who Williams's scouting reports should have told him homered twice in this very game—was who Williams wanted and Duda was who Williams got. Lucas doubled to left off Matt Thornton, scoring Granderson and pushing the Mets up, 3–2. Give Duda credit for the ribbie, but maybe circle the IBB to Cespedes as evidence that pitching to the Mets was going to be a whole new adventure. Nobody had been walking John Mayberry or Eric Campbell to get to Duda.

Familia followed on the heels of Bobby Parnell in the seventh and Robles in the eighth and threw a scoreless ninth. The Mets' pen was now unscored upon in seven-and-a-third innings in this series, the same series in which the Mets were undefeated and one game from first place.

* * *

The chance to forge a virtual tie (what's .0004623 between rivals?) played out under the *Sunday Night Baseball* spotlight, which ESPN viewers learned was made of unbreakable glass. If it hadn't been, the slugging Mets would have shattered it.

With one on and two out in the bottom of the third and the Mets trailing, 1–0, versus Jordan Zimmermann, the 2015 National League East's balance of power shifted once and for all. And by power, we mean Granderson homering to give the Mets a 2–1 lead; Daniel Murphy homering on the very next pitch to make it 3–1; Cespedes singling for his first Met hit; and Duda completing the inning's home run hat trick with a two-run bomb of his own.

The Mets were up, 5–1. All of Citi Field was a party deck now; the volume that was raised Friday night grew only louder as the series progressed. Once given the lead, Noah Syndergaard surrendered nothing more than a solo shot to Yunel Escobar. Thor went eight and struck out nine. Clippard finished up the 5–2 win to give the Met relief corps practically a complete game shutout for the weekend: 8 2/3 IP, 0 R.

While Terry Collins was able to count on Clippard in order to rest Familia en route to sweeping the Nationals and earning a share of first place, Williams never did get to use his old or new closer. There was no eighth-inning lead to hold, no ninth-inning situation to save. No Storen. No Papelbon. Strange that in a series with postseason implications he'd deploy neither of his major weapons, especially considering the Friday and Saturday games were settled late. The Washington general, however, insisted on hewing to rigidly defined roles.

That was going to be tough on him and his troops, for the Mets were about to recast the Nationals as a second-place team.

LOOK WHO'S NO. 1

How does that old chestnut go again? Oh right, like this:

Washington.

First in war.

First in peace.

And second in the National League East.

On August 3, one night after the Mets swept the Nationals out of Citi Field, they elbowed them out of any claim of first place in their division. New York traveled to Miami and pounded the Marlins, 12–1. Yoenis Cespedes collected three hits and Michael Conforto belted his first major league homer. Simultaneously in our nation's capital, the Arizona Diamondbacks held off the successors to the Senators, 6–4.

The Mets were alone in first place. They liked it so much, they began to decorate. It was predictable behavior, given the Mets' historical tendency to get to first and get downright cozy.

"LOOK WHO'S NO. 1," the Shea scoreboard suggested on September 10, 1969, the night the Mets nosed ahead of the Cubs. Those Mets kept their nose heading only one way from there: up. They weren't snobs, they just weren't giving up first place. Same thing happened in the five-team rumble for the NL East flag in 1973. They had four competitors right down to the wire, but once the Mets moved in on September 21, they never moved out. The '86 Mets took first place on April 22 and didn't think of giving it up. The '88 Mets waited until May 3 to become similarly proprietary. In

'06, the Mets didn't mess around much. They were in first as of April 6 and remained in first clear to the end of the season.

These Mets hadn't been as sure of themselves in their penthouse surroundings, exchanging keys with the Nationals on a couple of occasions and experimenting with life in second place. They must not have cared for it, because they were back in first. Besides, "these Mets" were practically a new proposition. There'd been no Conforto or Cespedes around when the Mets were vacating first in May and June. There weren't a load of 12–1 wins, either.

* * *

The good offensive times kept rolling for the Mets in Florida. They swept three from the Marlins—outscoring them 25–8—and then took a series-opener in St. Pete in which Conforto delivered a clutch ninth-inning double and Wilmer Flores the eventual game-winning double. The 4–3 victory over the Rays on August 7 extended the Mets' winning streak to seven. They hadn't lost since that day in the rain against the Padres, which seemed like a very long time ago.

Two one-run losses at Tampa Bay dimmed the Sunshine State road trip a bit, but the standings remained in good stead, with the Mets a game-and-a-half up on the Nationals as they flew home. A new winning streak commenced against the Rockies, who came into Citi Field for what turned into four more Met wins.

Four more raucous Mets wins, it should be noted. It's not so much that they buried last-place Colorado—only the last of the four was a blowout—but Citi Field stayed loud, supportive and engaged. Maybe that shouldn't have seemed worth mentioning, but from 2009 through 2014, even at intervals in 2015, the home of the Mets didn't engender much enthusiasm. It could be a nice place to visit, but sometimes it was hard to tell that your favorite ballclub lived there.

The Nationals series changed that and the Rockies series certified it. The third game of the set, in particular, transmitted a different tone. It was Colorado on a Wednesday night, which in previous years meant you could sit pretty much anywhere you liked and if you were in the mood to purchase a snack (something Citi Field specialized in selling you), you wouldn't have to wait long.

* * *

Why was this Wednesday night different from all other Wednesday nights? Maybe it was first place, maybe it was the momentum, maybe it was the critical mass of the Mets finally being the Mets we wanted them to be, but boy was it different. There were 37,175 of us in the building for baseball and nothing but baseball. No free shirts on a Wednesday. No quick visits to the concessions, either. And, for the first time I could recall, no sense of attention wandering. We were all there to watch and cheer the Mets.

We watched Jacob deGrom strike out 10 and give up only two hits across seven—and we cheered. We watched new Met Juan Uribe and nearly forgotten newish Met Michael Cuddyer (who handled his transition to part-time status with team-first grace) drive in runs in back-to-back at-bats in the fourth—and we cheered. We watched Cespedes in a neon yellow compression sleeve connect for his first Met home run—and goodness, did we cheer.

You could make out the sleeve from Promenade, though you probably had to be watching on television to notice a parakeet that perfectly accessorized Yoenis's accessory clinging to the screen behind home plate. The synergy was too perfect, and thus was born the Rally Parakeet. The bird matched our mood: bright.

If we'd seen our new avian mascot from where we were sitting, we would have cheered it, too.

* * *

The Mets won, 3–0. A fine win, certainly, but essentially just another win in an August when they were beginning to become regularly scheduled events. Of course we were happy. I just didn't realize how happy until I started to leave Citi Field.

I entered a staircase that takes you down to field level and heard something besides the shuffling of feet. I heard chanting. I heard "LET'S GO METS!" over and over again. That was a sound that I thought was left for the demolition crews when the last of the Shea Stadium ramps was torn down. Nope, it was as alive at Citi Field as it was constant, unyielding and celebratory. We were celebrating more than a win over Colorado, I was certain. We were celebrating more than the Mets' status as a first-place entity and the extension of their first-place lead (it would be up to three-and-a-half by night's end, four-and-a-half the next day). We were, I deduced, celebrating ourselves.

We were getting to be Mets fans again. We were getting to come to a ballgame and root for our ballclub and make ourselves heard and not feel that if we shouted, we were shouting into a vacuum. We were part of what the Mets were doing and it felt great to be doing it again. First-place, first-person plural wasn't delusional for those of us in the stands and on the stairs. This meant something to us, something a fan only understands when he or she has been without it for too long.

The traffic on the staircase was downward, but the direction at Citi Field was up, up and away.

OUT OF THIN AIR

When the Pirates replaced the Rockies on the Mets' dance card, tangoing became much more of a challenge. The Mets hadn't seen the Buccos since losing three straight to them in Pittsburgh in May and hadn't had much reason to think about them once the East supplanted the wild card as their access road to the postseason.

Trying to get to October through the Pirates would have been an onerous task. The Met juggernaut slowed for a series that culminated in three consecutive home defeats. But with the Nationals helpfully experiencing their own malaise on the West Coast, the weekend wasn't a total loss. The Mets learned some valuable lessons.

Like Michael Conforto could go deep at Citi Field; he notched his first home park homer in the Saturday game. Like Yoenis Cespedes could go deep from center field; he unleashed a line drive of a throw in the ninth that nailed Sean Rodriguez as the Buc baserunner mistakenly thought he could stretch a double into a triple. Like Bobby Parnell couldn't be considered a component of any late-inning plans Terry Collins was making for the rest of the season.

* * *

This was a difficult lesson to learn for anybody who had followed Parnell from the rawest of rookies in 2008 (he threw the last Met pitch ever thrown at Shea Stadium) up a strenuous learning curve and into his role as one of the league's more effective closers in 2013. Then came injuries, surgery, rehabilitation, and the hope that he could contribute to the back end of the bullpen now that Met games mattered like crazy.

Alas, Parnell couldn't get anybody out in the tenth inning on Friday night and undid Sunday afternoon's 1–1 tie in agonizing fashion, allowing four runs in the seventh. Bobby comes from a family of firefighters in North Carolina, which I figured was why he always looked like someone waiting for the worst to happen. In the context of what he could do for the 2015 Mets, he had just encountered it. Parnell wouldn't be called on to douse any more meaningful blazes for the rest of the year.

The Mets also learned that as well as their bullpen had performed in spots, it wasn't in the class of the Pirates, whose relievers shut them down with increasing ease from Friday to Sunday. That might have reflected more on the Met hitters, but the bullpen, despite the addition of Clippard and, more recently, lefty Eric O'Flaherty, was still a potential fire hazard.

After a split of two games in Baltimore—the loss, disturbingly enough from a relief standpoint, came when Carlos Torres surrendered a walk-off homer—the Mets traveled to Denver. The last thing anybody there thought about was pitching.

* * *

This was Coors Field before the humidor. This was Coors Field as if the Blake Street Bombers of 1995 were reanimated, reactivated and directed to the visitors' dugout in a Rocky Mountain High act of hospitality.

This was unbelievable, even at an altitude a mile in the air.

On Friday night, August 21, the Mets prevailed by a final of 14–9, a tally by which they'd never previously triumphed in their fifty-four years on the planet.

On Saturday night, August 22, they won by the exact same score. It was like being stopped in one's tracks by a unicorn one night and then bumping into the very same unicorn the next night. Or maybe the unicorn was cloned.

What baseball team wins consecutive 14–9 games? And who said you're never gonna see no uniclone?

* * *

It was one of the statistically quirkiest Go Figures of 2015. Elevation of 5,280 feet explains only so much. Yoenis Cespedes explains much of the rest. Cespedes's impact on the Mets' zeitgeist and lineup was already in place, but he hadn't exactly broken out before the Denver trip, batting .274 in 17 games, with a pair of homers and eight ribbies. In the two series preceding the set in Colorado, in which the Mets had won only one of five games, he'd driven in but a single run.

Well, the monster was out of the cage now.

Friday night, Yoenis doubled in the first and scored on Lucas Duda's single to make the score a very innocent 1–0. His second-inning grand slam gave the Mets a 7–1 lead, setting the tone for the rest of the night and weekend. When the Rockies crept to within 7–4, Cespedes led off the fourth with another home run. With the damn thing tied 8–8 in the sixth, *La Potencia* tapped Christian Friedrich for a two-run shot. In the eighth, an inning after Travis d'Arnaud and Conforto homered back-to-back, Peerless Yo from near Manzanillo (Cuba, that is) singled, advanced on a groundout and *stole third*—because you can never have too many runs in Coors Field—before coming home on Wilmer Flores's double.

While the Colorado pitching staff was presumably checking to see if the team's health insurance covered group therapy, Cespedes was signing off on one of the most gobsmacking performances in Mets history: three homers, a double, a single, five runs, seven RBIs and that stolen base. Edgardo Alfonzo once collected six hits in a game in which he homered three times. Carlos Delgado once drove in nine runs. Ten players from Jim Hickman to Scott Hairston had cycled. But nobody had ever seen a Met make the earth move the way Cespedes did that Friday night.

* * *

Yet everybody would see another 14–9 Mets win within twenty-four hours. Juan Uribe homered with no runner aboard in the third inning Saturday night; the other 13 runs would come without any Met going deep, which showed how Coors Field's keg could be popped from any number of angles. Three Mets had three hits, five others—Cespedes included—had two. Jon Niese (5 1/3 IP), like Bartolo Colon the evening before (3 2/3 IP), didn't particularly cotton to pitching in the thin air any more than their

Rockie counterparts, but this was a new era for Mets baseball. It was an era in which pitchers couldn't complain about was not getting enough runs with which to work.

Pitching was indeed the last thing anybody was thinking about at Coors Field, but it had definitely crossed Met minds on the way west, because a strategic decision had been made. Matt Harvey was skipped what would have been his turn Sunday afternoon. It was hard to remember by this point in the season, but technically Matt was still returning from a full year lost to rehabilitation from surgery. He was the co-ace of a first-place team and pitching like it most starts. Before 2015 began, there were murmurs about limiting his innings, but he'd looked so good and pitched so well that you could be forgiven for forgetting he was supposed to be handled at least a little with kid gloves.

Harvey was rested and Logan Verrett was called up from Las Vegas to start. As with most everything else these days, it worked out wonderfully for the Mets. Verrett went eight, struck out eight and won a relatively humdrum 5–1 decision to sweep the Rockies. The Mets had played seven series since trading for Cespedes and they'd swept four of them. It was a new era, indeed.

The time had come for an old Met to rejoin the fun.

ALL SPINE, NO STENOSIS

L ate August. Citizens Bank Park. Mets. Phillies.
     Shiver.

The Camelot we thought we'd be inhabiting once 2006 became 2006—
the Mets combining homegrown young talent with well-chosen acquisitions
to spectacular effect for years to come—began to disintegrate the week 2007
truly became 2007. That was the week the Mets went to Philadelphia for
four games and left with four losses. The experience dragged the first-place
Mets down a spiritual notch and raised the Phillies to the lip of serious contention. It would take a couple of more weeks for everything really start falling apart, as the Mets waited until mid-September to completely buckle, but
the Collapse of '07 was seeded and watered at the end of August.

Rooting for the Mets was never quite the same again. If you couldn't
trust your alleged big-deal team to swat away the first competitor to stick
its tongue out at them, how much faith you could reasonably invest? After
September 2007, the month that crashed to earth with 12 Met losses in 17
games while the Phillies were going 13–4 and stealing the East, I know I was
never quite the same again.

More than a division title was lost. My innocence went missing. I
became a very cynical Mets fan from 2008 on. When '08 wound down in
similar fashion, a playoff spot blown on the final day at home (and the final
day at Shea ever), the cynicism gripped me for the next half-decade and
then some. Even a few wins here and there didn't much stir me. *This is just
a setup,* I thought to myself. *Why waste good cheering on such a bad team anyway? Save the wins for a year when it matters.*

* * *

I eventually got over it . . . in 2015, a year that mattered. That's how long 2007 lingered in the depths of my soul; that's how badly I needed a wholly uplifting season to come along and delete the ill will from eight years before.

On paper, the behemoth Mets of 2015—11 over .500 and five ahead of the Nationals—arrived in Philadelphia for a four-game series on August 24 much as the Mets of 2007—17 over, six up—had. In spirit, almost everything was different.

Why shouldn't it be? Eight years shouldn't have felt recent. Eight years before 1986 was 1978 and nobody invoked the 1978 Mets in 1986. Goodness knows the last-place Phillies were no longer any kind of threat. Other than the time-ravaged Carlos Ruiz and physically diminished Ryan Howard, the Phillies who made the Mets' lives miserable during their divisional dynasty of '07 to '11 had all scattered. The Phlagship Phillies, their double play combination of Jimmy Rollins and Chase Utley, were among the last to leave. They were still working together, but now in LA Rollins had signed with the Dodgers in the offseason and Utley had just joined him. The Dodgers were in a race. The Phillies were going nowhere.

As for the 2007 Mets, what could you say about them in 2015 that John Cusack as Buck Weaver didn't say in the final scene of *Eight Men Out*? Buck, sitting in the grandstand in Hoboken, told some younger fans who were pretty sure they were watching Shoeless Joe Jackson of the disgraced Black Sox play under an assumed identity that they must be mistaken. "Those fellas," Buck informed them, "are all gone now."

The same held true for the 2007 Mets who made us wish what they did wasn't so. Except for one. He'd been gone most of 2015, but as the Mets prepared to play ball in Philadelphia, he was listed in their lineup, playing third, batting fourth, and wearing five.

* * *

David Wright was back. Even his back, a victim of the now notorious spinal stenosis, was back. Technically, he was never gone. Having been a Met and nothing but a Met since July 21, 2004, had distinguished him from his peers. No active player who'd been tethered to one team for his entire career had totaled more plate appearances than Wright. No National Leaguer had been with one team longer. Rollins held that distinction until 2015. Utley had taken it until three days before. Once he wrapped himself in Dodger blue, no NL player could say he'd been anything as long as Wright had been a Met.

Wright hadn't been a Met in a game since April 14. It wasn't as long ago as July of '04 or August of '07, but it represented a lengthy absence. David used the time to effectively exercise the back in hopes of returning to the pursuit of his and the Mets' first playoff appearance since October '06.

General MacArthur once proclaimed of the Philippines, "I Shall Return." Captain Wright was more of a low-key character, but his statement upon taking Philadelphia surely resounded in its realm.

On Monday night the 24th, Wright returned. Wow, did he return. It was the second inning, the Mets down, 3–0, on a three-run homer from Howard; it was the last echo of the bad old days the Mets would hear at Citizens Bank. Wright led off the inning and launched a laser to left in his first at-bat in more than four months. The ball carried to the second deck of the ballpark and into the heart of every Mets fan. Wright, the player who didn't want to play anywhere else, was now playing for a first-place team. The fun started without him, but he was here to join in on it and, where it counted tonight, to lead it.

Talk about leading by example. Although David admitted he was ready to pull "a Wilmer Flores" on the field, there wasn't much time to get emotional. Wright's homer off Adam Morgan was a necessary shot not just in the arm but on the scoreboard. Citizens Bank hadn't become less of a bandbox in his absence. To the contrary, Home Run Derby was playing out in Philadelphia and early on, the Phillies were winning at it. Cameron Rupp and Domonic Brown guided their own missiles over the fence, dwarfing the impact of the solo shot Juan Lagares sent flying. After three innings, the Phillies had outhomered the Mets, 3–2, and led them, 7–2.

That was about to change.

* * *

Flores homered with Wright on first in the fourth to make it 7–4.
Travis d'Arnaud homered behind him to make it 7–5.

Flores dropped a three-run bomb in the fifth to give the Mets an 8–7 lead.
Michael Cuddyer, two batters later, added a solo statement; 9–7.
Daniel Murphy homered with a man on in the sixth; 11–7.
D'Arnaud doubled (piker) two more home in the same inning; 13–7.
Lagares singled home a run in the seventh; 14–7.
Yoenis Cespedes . . . two-run home run in the ninth; 16–7.

For those who were now trained to spot Unicorn Scores after Denver, there was another one to mount on the wall. The Mets had never won a 16–7 game before. Now they had. If it wasn't the most famous 16–7 score in New York sports history—Joe Namath led the Jets to victory in Super Bowl III by those numbers—it was certainly guaranteed to shake up the Met record books.

Eight Met home runs. That was a record.

Fifteen extra-base hits. That was a record, too.

Most rubbing of eyes in wonderment? Probably set on August 24, but the Mets had been revising the experiential section of their records on a regular basis all month, so just jot that one down in pencil.

* * *

Tuesday night's game was won by a more baseball-ish score, 6–5. Cespedes homered again. Noah Syndergaard doubled in two runs. Hansel Robles brewed a bit of a firestorm by quick-pitching Darin Ruf. Two Phillies who'd been Mets—Jeff Francoeur and coach Larry Bowa—complained to the umpires that their batter wasn't ready to be pitched to. If Ruf's head is down, he can't see what might be coming toward him, the danger to the hitter outweighing any advantage the pitcher was seeking. It could be Francoeur and Bowa (who was ejected) had a legitimate point. Or it could have been their frustration boiling over.

The Mets, however, weren't done frustrating them. On Wednesday night, Cuddyer homered and drove in three, Cespedes scored a couple more times and the Mets cruised to a 9–4 triumph. And on Thursday . . .

Well, Thursday was interesting. Jon Niese was strafed for five runs in the third inning, but as was their habit, the Mets strafed back. "Boom," went the d'Arnaud might in the fourth, cutting the deficit to 5–2. Two more rounds of artillery were exploded in the fifth, one from Cespedes and one from Kelly Johnson, knotting the game at five.

It stayed there for a while, with the Mets leaving a runner or more on base in every inning from the sixth through the ninth. Their bullpen was an immovable object in the meantime and extra innings unfolded. All threats were brushed aside over the next three innings, with one Phillies attempt at landing a baserunner meeting an unconventional doom.

* * *

In the bottom of the tenth with two out, Carlos Torres entered the game to pitch (not too quickly, lest Bowa gripe) to Francoeur. Frenchy sent a bolt up the middle that ricocheted off Torres's left foot. It caromed toward first base, where Murphy—playing there in place of the injured Lucas Duda—corralled it and, on the off chance somebody would swing by to catch it, flung it to first with his back toward home plate. Torres had kept running the whole time and arrived at precisely the right moment and angle to receive Daniel's fling-and-a-prayer. He beat Francoeur to the bag for the 1-3-1 putout.

If McDonald's was considering rebooting its 1990s Michael Jordan-Larry Bird ad campaign, they could have done worse than signing Daniel and Carlos on the spot.

Off the pitcher's foot
Bounces to Murphy
Desperation toss to Torres
Nothing but Met

* * *

There was so much to like folded into that "play of the year," as Gary Cohen called it. Consider Murphy starting at first base in Duda's absence. If Terry Collins needed Daniel somewhere, he went there. The same guy who worked at second base until he became adequate shifted to third when Wright wasn't around for a long stretch. Now he was a first baseman until told otherwise. It's one thing for a utilityman to be that versatile. But Daniel Murphy was no Super Joe McEwing. He was a regular—a regular twice over. He started more games at second (65) than any Met in 2015 and more games at third (41). And by throwing in 14 starts at first, you wound up with a defensive profile unlike that of any regular in Mets history. Murphy wasn't the greatest fielder on the premises, but he always found a way to keep his bat in the lineup.

As for Carlos Torres, his co-starring role in a highlight-reel staple brought him a wave of attention that he probably deserved just for staying power. Carlos joined the Mets' active roster in the middle of June 2013 and hadn't been off it since for any reason. No DL, no demotion, no paternal or bereavement leave, no leave at all, not even to check his messages or grab a quick smoke. No Met at the moment had maintained an active-duty streak anywhere near as long. "I'm sort of a permanent fixture," John McGraw once told Grantland Rice after nearly three decades of managing the New York Giants. "Like home plate and the flag pole." But even McGraw handed over managing duties for extended periods due to illness.

Torres was Mr. Fixture. He'd pitched in short roles, long roles, occasionally as a starter. He accepted the absurd uniform number of 72 so Cespedes could feel at home in Carlos's old 52. Oh, and he could hit, which would become abundantly clear in the top of the 13th.

Torres stayed in after his and Murphy's acrobatic act and kept the Phillies off the board through the 11th and 12th. Terry, short of reserves by now, let him lead off the 13th. Carlos beat out an infield single and then sprinted to second on Curtis Granderson's single (we'd already learned the pitcher could run). One out later, Murphy came up and doubled both runners home.

The Mets were being the Mets again, and the Phillies were helpless to stop it. Michael Conforto would eventually single in another couple of runs and the Mets would win, 9–5. It was their seventh straight win and another series sweep, this one of the four-game variety. Four games captured in late August at Citizens Bank Park . . . a stinging rebuke at last to the way the Mets went down eight late Augusts before in the very same space.

* * *

In contemporary terms, David Wright and the Mets had stretched their division lead to six-and-a-half games over fading Washington. In the context of signs and omens, Torres's offensive prowess (which, like the 1-3-1 put-out, manifested itself on the 29th anniversary of the Lenny Dykstra to John Gibbons to Howard Johnson game-ender Tim McCarver immortalized in San Diego with his call of "out at home . . . out at third . . . your basic 8-2-5 double play."), served as a more subtle marker for where the Mets could soon be headed.

By leading off the 13th with a hit and coming around to cross the plate with the go-ahead run, Torres became the first Met relief pitcher in franchise history to do exactly that in extra innings. No Met reliever had led off an inning after the ninth with a single (or something greater) and scored any run, let alone the winning run. In fact, no Met reliever had scored a run in extra innings since Roger McDowell did it at Pittsburgh in 1988. McDowell doubled with one out, so he wasn't quite the Rickey Henderson-brand catalyst Torres proved to be.

Only four Met relievers prior to Torres had ever scored a run in extra innings. The last one before McDowell was his 1986 partner in saves, Jesse Orosco. And whose likeness was coming to Citi Field two days hence in bobblehead form? Why, Jesse Orosco's. The first 15,000 of us in the park on Saturday would be handed a tiny Jesse, his knees on the ground, his fists in the air, a world championship in his firm grasp.

Those sorts of giveaways used to make me wistful for the seasons and successes they celebrated. This one felt like a masterstroke of synergy. 2015 might not yet belong in the same conversation as 1986, but it sure as hell spoke louder than the failures of 2007.

HOW WE GOT
TO THE PLAYOFFS

SURPRISES

A baseball season carries with it the capacity to surprise you 162 times. It's counterintuitive that you can get to late August and not know what's coming. But there's always something.

In the 129th game of 2015, I arrived ridiculously early at Citi Field for my Jesse Orosco bobblehead only to discover long, long lines snaking out in every direction. So much for sophisticated New Yorkers showing up fashionably late or not being impressed by mere trinkets. I attended John Franco Bobblehead Night in 2013 and they literally couldn't give them all away—and John's the pride of Bensonhurst.

Was ceramic Jesse that much of a draw twenty-nine years after his signature moment? Did the last-place Red Sox from the other league evoke that much interest? How much 1986 nostalgia was in the air anyway? I found a line that didn't overly intimidate, stood firm against potential interlopers (why would Boston fans want a reminder of the moment they lost that World Series?), and got my bobblehead. I even got another omen for my collection. The Mets had lost to the Red Sox at home the night before. They lost again on this Saturday. The last time they lost two straight games to the Red Sox in Queens, they went on to win it all.

Talk about projecting one's 1986 instincts. There was no telling on August 29 where an omen could take you, but the Mets did win the finale of the series at hand on Sunday the 30th, capturing one of three from Boston, and they did pick up another reliever in their ongoing effort to calm their bullpen anxieties. The prize in this case was Addison Reed from Arizona, formerly a closer, now perhaps the seventh-inning bridge from the starter to Tyler Clippard. Clippard was still being counted on to set up Jeurys Familia, who would be due a bobblehead day of his own in 2044 if everybody did his job beautifully and the newly established Orosco Precedent held.

* * *

In the 131st game of 2015, Ruben Tejada took an unforeseen trip from home plate to home plate without a baseball ever leaving the field of play. Ruben hit himself an inside-the-park home run in a 9–4 clobbering of the Phillies at Citi Field. Outside-the-park homers had never been his thing— he slid into third during the first he hit at Wrigley in 2010, unconvinced he had actually gone deep—so if Ruben was going to get four bases on one swing, it was going to take some fancy lack of fielding for it to happen.

It was the bottom of the second on Wednesday, September 2. Aaron Nola was pitching. Kelly Johnson was on second, having doubled in David Wright, who had singled. Tejada was working a full count, as was his wont during his 2012 heyday, when 239 feet of Statcast-measured magic unfurled. Tejada swung and served a fair ball midway down the right field line. Domonic Brown had a vague idea about backhanding it but instead tumbled into Albert Achievement Awards territory by flipping head over heels over the lethally low nearby side wall. With the right fielder out of commission (and ultimately out for the season in deference to concussion concerns), the ball was free to keep rolling, meaning Ruben was free to keep running. Second baseman Cesar Hernandez scurried into the corner to retrieve the ball; when an infielder finds himself deep in the outfield, it likely indicates the ball is a lost cause for the defense. Tejada slid into home out of habit, but scored unchallenged for the 27th inside-the-parker in the fifty-four-year history of the Mets. That averages out to one every two years, thought that sounds more frequent than they feel.

* * *

In the 135th game of 2015, Bartolo Colon . . . should anything be a surprise when it involves Bartolo Colon? That Bartolo Colon was a stalwart in an otherwise young-gun rotation eighteen years after first making a major league staff should have been the surprising aspect of his career, but after nearly two full seasons of Colon doing it all and doing it well, what was left to be shocked by?

Maybe the defense he flashed in the sixth inning at Marlins Park on Saturday night September 5. It wasn't that Bartolo made the play. We were always being reminded, a bit patronizingly, that Bartolo is quite the athlete for a man of his shall we say proportions. Justin Bour, a lumbering fellow in his own right, had tapped a ball down the first base line. Colon hustled from the mound to pick it up. Bour was between Bartolo and the bag. It didn't shape up as a difficult play but the path between himself and first baseman Eric Campbell was not unimpeded. There was a rumbling Bour right in the middle. So Colon circumvented it, flipping the ball behind his back without even a glance toward Campbell. He retired the runner with ease, grace, verve, panache, anything you like. "It's so easy for Colon right now, that he's able to put some mustard on it!" Gary Cohen affirmed. It was certainly the tastiest item on the Mets' menu all weekend; after taking two of three from the Phillies, the Mets dropped two of three to the Marlins, the Bartolo Spectacular representing the team's lone win. Colon threw a complete game shutout, the only one the Mets racked up in all of 2015.

The Mets were famously careful with their pitchers, though to one observer's analysis, not careful enough in a particular case. That observer had a vested interest in how the case in question played out.

* * *

Matt Harvey's comeback season was fairly sensational. Through his most recent start versus Philadelphia, he was 12–7 with an ERA of 2.60. The number of actual bad starts he'd thrown could easily fit inside the palm of your hand. If he wasn't quite dominating the National League as he did before Tommy John surgery, he was coming damn close. Once in a while, when his command or control was just a bit off, he reminded me of those old TVs when the picture wasn't quite right. You'd fiddle with the knobs, you'd shift the rabbit ears, you'd give the set a little zetz to on its side, yet it wouldn't necessarily tune in the way you wanted it to just because you wanted it to. The lesson was maybe you couldn't force some things.

Harvey had gone into the shop and come back as close to as good as new as we could reasonably ask for, but sometimes his big picture would come in a little snowy, a little jumpy, not exactly crisp. The sense extended to the pitcher's persona as much as his performance. I'd find myself thinking back to the Matt Harvey with whom we all fell in baseball love. I'd think of those first starts in 2012, when if he gave up two runs, he'd berate himself because the Mets scored only one, and one should have been enough for him. If the Mets scored no runs, then he insisted his job was to keep them in the game by putting up zeroes. It was unrealistic, but it was endearing.

No pitcher could put that much pressure on himself and succeed across the long term, but when 2012 became 2013, we got the sense that Matt Harvey could do anything he set his mind and his right arm to. He put up zeroes almost exclusively. He allowed his team every chance to win, and for a while the Mets never lost when he pitched. He threw an almost perfect game while his nose bled. It was revealed he stared down a bully of a veteran teammate who tried to pull rank. When he needed a run, he drove it in himself. We created a cause around him and we rallied to it.

That idealized memory probably clouded our interpretation of the events emanating from Miami in early September when Harvey's agent, Scott Boras, began leaking word he wasn't happy with how the Mets were handling his client. According to Boras, the Mets weren't supposed to allow Harvey to throw more than 180 innings in 2015. Harvey's total was 166 1/3 IP. There was a month of baseball remaining for sure, as much as another month in addition if everything broke right. Was Boras really saying the Mets should implement a Stephen Strasburg-style shutdown?

Strasburg, another Boras client who underwent Tommy John, was handled so carefully by the Nationals in 2012 that they sat him for his own good in that year's postseason. Without Strasburg, the Nats exited in the first round. The Mets, like those Nats, had plenty of other talented starting pitchers, but Harvey, like Strasburg, stood at the front of the line. They had been careful with Harvey—never once letting him complete a game, implementing ad hoc six-man rotations and skipping him entirely in Colorado— all in the name of making sure he'd be available in the heat of September and the heart of October.

Now Boras was intimating something different was cooking, and what made his pronouncements loom as more than irritating agentspeak was

Harvey not forcefully refuting him. We wanted Matt to say nothing more than, "Give me the ball." Instead, when pressed, he equivocated. Apparently Boras had not gone rogue; Harvey was complicit in expressing doubt about how much the Mets should use him the rest of the way. He was a young man with a career beyond 2015 to keep in mind. A healthy Harvey figured to clean up in a couple of years when he was eligible to hit the open market. A person could understand his reticence to put that in danger.

A fan, though, wasn't quite so worried about a pitcher's earning potential. A fan wanted his team's No. 1 or 1A starter (depending on how you chose to order Harvey and Jacob deGrom, the latter of whom had been less than his sharpest of late) to let nothing get in the way of winning his team a division title and then some. Since there'd been no public indication that anything was physically wrong with Harvey, a fan could be surprised to the point of blindsided that with the biggest series of the year waiting on the other side of the weekend this was suddenly an issue.

It wasn't a harmonious note on which to leave Miami and head toward Washington for the three games that had the potential to decide or derail the course of the 2015 season.

THE SOUND OF
ONE TEAM RACING

Whose bright idea was it to send the Washington Nationals the gift of a four-game home series against the Atlanta Braves? By September, the comatose Braves were making the Phillies look lively by comparison, practically begging to be let into the National League East basement. The Braves preceded the Mets as guests of the Nationals and they were distressingly polite. They lost all four games at Nationals Park, extending their own losing streak to 12 and allowing the Nats to pick up significant ground on the Mets. As the Mets showed up on Labor Day, September 7, to commence their three-game showdown, their lead over second-place Washington was trimmed to four games, the slightest margin they'd held since August 19.

For the first time since Yoenis Cespedes was a Detroit Tiger, momentum was not necessarily in the Mets' corner. The Nats were on a five-game winning streak, while the Mets had lost two of their three games at Miami in distressing walk-off fashion. Plus there was the innings-limit cloud seeded by Scott Boras and Matt Harvey. The Mets were trying to cooperate with their star pitcher and announced a tentative plan of withholding him here and there in September so they could get at least something out of him come October.

First, October had to come. To bring that elusive month to Citi Field, the Mets—behind Jon Niese on Monday, Harvey on Tuesday, and Jacob deGrom on Wednesday—were going to have to keep their lead from being whittled any further in September.

Niese wasn't really the man you wanted charged with keeping a hot team at bay (his ERA in his last four starts: 8.46), but it was his turn in the rotation and his agent wasn't pestering anybody about how many innings he should throw. The Mets hoped he'd throw a whole bunch of good ones.

* * *

The Mets found their long ball groove against Max Scherzer in the second, when Michael Conforto and Kelly Johnson each took the Nats' ace deep. The 2–0 lead rose to 3–0 in the fourth, when Yoenis Cespedes added his own solo shot.

Niese, staked to a comfortable lead, gave it up in four batters' time . . . the next four he faced. Two singles and a walk loaded the bases and Wilson Ramos, who came out of the womb with a grudge of some sort against the Mets, launched a grand slam. Three batters later, Jayson Werth doubled in another run. Niese was gone with one out in the fourth and the Mets were down by two.

Scherzer was supposed to be Bryce Harper's ticket to a World Series ring, at least in Harper's view. He'd been brought in to make a formidable pitching staff impenetrable. The Mets had beaten him twice early in the season, but he hadn't pitched badly against them. Matt Williams hadn't done anything special to get him into the games the clubs played in July and August. Now he was leaning on Scherzer to lead the Nats into this series. He was the one in the lead now. If there was going to be a ring in Harper's immediate future, today would be the day for Scherzer to start fitting him in earnest for it.

Somebody must have forgotten his jeweler's glass. Scherzer was no more effective pitching with a lead than Niese had been. Curtis Granderson drove in a run in the fifth. Travis d'Arnaud did the same in the sixth to tie the game. Scherzer gave up five runs in six innings. The rings would have to wait.

* * *

Niese's shortcomings were compensated for by a Mets bullpen that came to their teammate's aid. Carlos Torres untangled the mess he inherited in the fourth and was holding the fort in the fifth until his durability finally gave out following a 1-3 play of a far more routine nature than the one he executed with Daniel Murphy in Philadelphia. Torres exited with a strained left calf and Erik Goeddel took over for him, completing the fifth and steering the ship for two outs in the sixth before call-up Dario Alvarez was asked to come in and face his first batter of 2015: Bryce Harper.

The lefty-lefty matchup worked in the Mets' favor. Alvarez struck out Harper.

Bullpen management didn't necessarily figure to be Terry Collins's trump card, but his relievers weren't giving up any runs. When Williams gave it a whirl, the results were much the same . . . in the sense that they were friendly to the Mets.

* * *

Blake Treinen replaced Scherzer. Wilmer Flores singled; Ruben Tejada bunted him to second.

Felipe Rivero replaced Treinen. Granderson walked.

Casey Janssen replaced Rivero. David Wright singled Tejada home and Granderson to third; the Mets led, 6–5.

Matt Thornton replaced Janssen. Daniel Murphy's fly to left scored Granderson; Cespedes doubled home Wright; the Mets led, 8–5.

Four National relievers. Three Met runs. One hellacious fist pump out of Wright after he crossed the plate. *Yes,* it seemed to shout, *this is what all that stretching and exercising the back was for . . . this is what I signed that long-term deal for . . . this is what it's all frigging about.*

Even when filling David Wright's thought bubble, I can't imagine The Captain cursing.

* * *

Hansel Robles handled the seventh and eighth. Jeurys Familia was on for the ninth. The Mets had themselves a Labor Day picnic, putting an extra length between themselves and their pursuers. The 8–5 victory gave them a five-game lead heading into what couldn't help but be the strangest Harvey Day yet.

It would be lovely to report Matt brushed aside all the doubts, just as he had in the same ballpark five months before when he returned to the mound for the first time since 2013. Harvey, through all his phumpering to the press, had insisted, "I'm focused on Tuesday." Tuesday was here. Where would Harvey be?

Forgotten by the time it was over. And for Matt Harvey to be relegated to footnote status in his first start after the Great Innings Limit Ruckus of 2015, you know something much bigger had to have happened.

It did. The Mets did. They happened like crazy all over the Nationals.

Make no mistake, Harvey wasn't very good. Whether he was overly distracted (he'd gone so far as to declare in a bylined *Players' Tribune* article that he intended to pitch in the playoffs should the Mets get so far) or the Nats simply had his number, he didn't make it through six. The crowning blow was one of those veritable "little league home runs" Ron Darling's always talking about. The bases were loaded, the Mets were down by two and Michael Taylor singled. Here came every runner in creation to score, including Taylor, whose progress was aided immeasurably by a misplay in center from Cespedes (Yoenis's outfield dynamism had a way of taking the briefest of holidays).

The Nats led 7–1. Harvey was routed. Everything was going the Nationals' way.

Then it wasn't.

* * *

Wright, who had homered off Jordan Zimmermann in the second, led off the visitors' seventh with a single. Two outs followed before Conforto walked. Flores singled David home and Michael to third. Williams, 2014 National League Manager of the Year, commenced managing. He replaced Treinen with Rivero to face Kelly Johnson, who was pinch-hitting for Goeddel, who had replaced Harvey. Collins, in turn, substituted Juan Uribe for Johnson once Rivero entered.

You knew it was September, both from the whiplash changes and the number of bodies available. And you knew once Rivero walked Uribe to load the bases and Granderson to force in Conforto that Williams maybe wasn't going to make it two consecutive Manager of the Year awards.

Out went Rivero. In came Drew Storen, the Nats' former closer, now their eighth-inning man. Williams was using him in the seventh because the eighth inning might not matter if the Mets' threat wasn't quashed immediately. It was 7–3, Nationals, but if a team with a four-run lead could be understandably looking over its shoulder, it was this one.

Cespedes was up next. Whatever afflicted him in the field when he whiffed on Taylor's single surely wasn't bothering him now. He lashed a double down the left field line that cleared the bases and brought the Mets to within 7–6. Storen stayed on to walk Daniel Murphy, uncork a wild pitch to move the runners to second and third, walk Wright and, finally, walk Lucas Duda.

It was 7–7. Harvey was off the hook. The Nationals were bolted to it.

* * *

Addison Reed, obtained by the Mets to stabilize the latter innings, pitched a scoreless seventh. Jonathan Papelbon, acquired to nail down victories, was asked to preserve a tie. After getting two outs, he was tasked with facing the .192-batting Kirk Nieuwenhuis, who'd missed all of August with an injury. He'd had only three ABs in September and, despite the pleasant memory of those three homers he hit at Citi Field just before the All-Star break, wasn't necessarily a prime candidate to put his stamp on a pennant race.

Kirk nominated himself anyway. In Washington sometimes the only way to fill a job is by executive order. On a 1–0 count, he hereby declared Papelbon would give up a home run of the highest order. He took the erstwhile All-Star over the right field fence, broke a tie for the Mets and the backs of their rivals.

Clippard and Familia threw zeroes in the eighth and ninth. The Mets won, 8–7, expanding their lead to six games and presenting an opportunity, in Wednesday night's finale, to put away their competition and division once and for all.

* * *

That chance would happily land on the 46th anniversary of the Black Cat Game. On September 9, 1969, at Shea Stadium, the Cubs saw a notorious symbol of bad luck cross in front of their dugout. On September 9, 2015, the Nationals might have noticed a shattered mirror or two in theirs.

Or was it enough to have seen who was in the other dugout?

For the third consecutive game, the Nationals led for a spell. For the third consecutive game, the Mets eventually cast a more effective spell. DeGrom (9 SO) and Strasburg (13 SO) battled through seven, Strasburg holding a 2–1 lead until the eighth. Collins chose Johnson to pinch-hit for Flores to lead off the inning. There was no great sabermetric motivation for it. Terry said he was playing a hunch.

Some hunch. Johnson homered to tie the Wednesday night game at two. One out later, Granderson singled, forcing Williams's hand. He went to Storen in his reluctantly adopted native habitat, the eighth, to take on Cespedes. Finally, the Matt in the Nat hat would have the reliever he wanted pitching in the inning he purposefully slotted him.

The next sound you heard was a Nat going "splat!" Who needed a black cat when everything Washington touched turned to mold?

* * *

Storen threw, but it was Cespedes who delivered, whacking the two-run home run that put the Mets ahead, 4–2. *"It's goin' for a ride!"* Howie Rose alerted everybody listening over WOR. *"It's not comin' back!"* Rarely had a dramatic blow seemed so preordained. This was the Mets' series to win. The fact that they trailed in all three of the games seemed incidental in hindsight.

After the half-inning was over, Storen promptly retreated to the Nationals clubhouse and took his frustrations out on his locker. His locker wasn't impressed. Storen wound up breaking his right thumb and was done for the season.

Just like the Nationals, more or less. Harper did hit his second solo home run of the evening in the bottom of the eighth, but Conforto answered directly with an RBI single. Familia pitched a 1-2-3 ninth to make it a 5–3 Mets win.

Hmmm . . . 5–3 was the score by which the Mets beat the Orioles to end the 1969 World Series . . . and 8–5, which was what the Mets won by on Monday, was the score by which the Mets topped the Red Sox to clinch the 1986 World Series. The coincidences and comparisons didn't seem so fanciful anymore. The first-place 2015 Mets led the National League East by seven games with 23 to play.

Their magic number was 17. Their magic was indisputable.

INCHING TOWARD CLINCHING

"You've gotta be kidding me! This team just doesn't know how to lose!" That was Gary Cohen making an informed inference regarding the New York Mets' knowledge base as it stood in the ninth inning on Sunday, September 13, 2015. The Mets appeared as close to losing as they had since departing Miami a week earlier. They'd taken those three crucial games from the increasingly irrelevant Nats, and then three from the plummeting Braves. The fourth in the latter series, at Turner Field, appeared to be the bone a first-place club throws a thoroughly dispirited also-ran when no real harm comes from an isolated defeat. Atlanta led, 7–4, heading to the ninth. They hadn't won a home game since August 24. I actually caught myself feeling some kind of weird simpatico for however many hundreds of Braves fans who'd paid their way in for this game. I knew what it was like to sit through a terrible September in my ballpark as the contenders blew through town. *Ah*, I thought, *let 'em have this one.*

Glad the Mets didn't hear my nonsensical thinking. What happened next was so much more fulfilling. To paraphrase the long-ago decree of Larry "Chipper" Jones, let the Braves fans go home and put on their NAS-CAR stuff.

* * *

It didn't matter what I thought. Like Gary said, the Mets didn't know how to lose. That much became evident when, with two out and nobody on in the top of the ninth, Juan Lagares doubled just out of the reach of Cameron Maybin; Curtis Granderson walked; and Daniel Murphy blasted the three-run homer that showed how little the Mets understood about the concept of defeat. The game was tied at seven and untied in the top of the 10th on a single, an error and four walks. The Mets went on to win, 10–7, ensuring (as if there'd been any doubt) their first winning season in seven years.

Once more, the Mets swept a series from a National League East opponent. It may be that nobody else in their division—which they now led by nine-and-a-half—knew how to win, but you play who you play and the Mets were playing everybody for keeps. The next night, when they beat the Marlins at Citi Field, they were the proud owners of 31 wins in 42 games; 31–11 was exactly how the 1986 Mets started their season. The 2015 team was 83–61 overall, marking the first time any band of Mets had climbed 22 games above .500 since 2006.

* * *

Everybody was contributing to the lack of losing, but one Met was responsible for the biggest chunk. From the day the Mets acquired Yoenis Cespedes, they were a different team. That was when 31–11 started. That was when Met seasons that had had postseasons attached to them began seeping into our conversations. Cespedes, despite the brevity of his Met tenure, was stirring National League MVP talk. On one hand, it was absurd. He'd been a Met for less than seven weeks. On the other hand, what a seven-week engagement it was.

Donn Clendenon was a revered figure in Met history, the archetype of the ideal deadline pickup. Clendenon was the in-season missing piece in 1969. He strengthened a young lineup, made them legit, helped lead them to the promised land right away, even won the World Series MVP. Every year at the trade deadline, if the Mets were on the cusp of any kind of contention, we yearned for another Clendenon.

Cespedes was the modern Met-ric equivalent of four Clendenons.

Once Yoenis started belting home runs, it seemed he'd never stop. His first one flew out of Citi Field on August 12. His 17th took flight on September 14. Seventeen home runs would have led nine previous Met squads for entire seasons. Most of those were lousy Met teams, but that was part of the point. The team Cespedes had been leading through August and September and toward October was the diametric opposite of lousy . . . which aficionados of *I Love Lucy* will immediately identify as "swell."

How valuable, to say nothing of swell, were those shells Cespedes fired over fences from New York to Denver and back? Consider that only four of the Cespedes Seventeen were launched in Met losses—which made sense, considering how these Mets, per Mr. Cohen, no longer knew how to lose.

* * *

Unfortunately, they began to remember in the middle of September. It probably wasn't coincidental that their memory for losing started to kick in a bit on the night Cespedes took a ball off his hip from Miami's Tom Koehler. It wasn't an obviously physically damaging HBP, but it appeared Yoenis had his mojo dinged. The man had been all mojo to that point.

The Mets lost two in a row to the Marlins, two of three to the Yankees, then two of three to the Braves, all at home. It was a statistical correction, a human response. Few teams keep up a 31–11 pace; even the 1986 stepped back after their .738 start and finished the year with a mere .667 winning percentage. Only problem in 2015 was we'd gotten used to almost never losing and we were getting antsy to clinch.

It would have been nice to have done so at Citi Field, but the Mets lost just enough and the Nationals won just enough to send the potential celebration on the road. If there was an upside to the Mets' recent fallibility at home, it was the contrast it presented vis-à-vis how much they had improved away from Queens. Since Cespedes came aboard, the Mets were a 20–5 road team. With their magic number down to five, they packed for Cincinnati to begin a four-game series on Thursday night, September 24.

Great American Ball Park was as good a place as any to remember to forget how to lose.

OUR TEAM, OUR TIME

One of the most splendid benefits of counting down to your team's inevitable division title—and I was willing to count the 2015 NL East flag as in the bag, if not fully Ziploc-sealed when the Mets alighted in Cincinnati holding a six-and-a-half-game lead with 10 to play—is you are granted time to think about What It All Means, especially if it's been a while since you were permitted to so indulge.

Mets fans hadn't had one of these babies land on their doorstep in nine years. There was nothing old hat about the sensation. You were entitled to contemplate.

I was happy for myself, naturally. I was in my forty-seventh year of rooting for the Mets. This was only the eighth time I'd be seeing my team qualify for the playoffs, only the sixth time they'd be crowned divisional champs en route. I'm not made of stone, so yes, of course this one was good for me.

But it wouldn't be much fun if I was the only one happy about it. I was happy that it made others happy. I was happy for those who'd shared this passion as long as I'd held mine, if not longer. Those of us with nineteen sixty something on our birth certificates literally grew up with the Mets, and though we don't get extra credit for it, there's something about that demographic bond that keeps us feeling particularly close to our baseball team. I might never get used to the idea that forever more there will be moments in Metsdom that happened "fifty years ago today," but it puts into perspective how the Mets and we have been together practically forever.

Length of tenure isn't everything, though. You come along when you come along and if you fell into the Mets at a young age, whenever your youth happened to be, then you've been at it long enough. You deserved the happiness of the Mets' eighth playoff berth even if you missed the first two or four or more.

And if you missed every era that preceded the current epoch, then bless you and take a bow. You might have been born at a juncture that precluded you from knowing not just 1969 and 1973 and/or 1986 and 1988, but maybe 1999 and 2000. You could be foggy on 2006. Time marches on and clears a path for those who wouldn't know from Miracles and You Gotta Believe except as *Mets Yearbook* rain delay theater. Your Mets experience could have begun with a collapse and meandered below .500. You never had to get used to Citi Field because Citi Field is the only Mets ballpark you've ever known. Yet you were still a Mets fan. My goodness, I was happy you were about to find out what all the fuss was about.

If you came to the Mets later in life—by marriage, by immigration, by one day looking up at the television and deciding that team on the screen was somehow for you—then your elation is every bit as earned as mine. The Mets may extract blood, sweat and tears from you, but you don't have to fill out a form to prove your loyalty (they tried that with the "True New Yorker" marketing gambit of 2014 and it backfired blazingly). Adult conversions are welcome. They're admirable. We know you had your choice of baseball teams and we thank you for flying with us.

* * *

So I'm happy for the entire family of fan at the moment of impending clinch. There's something in it for each of us and it's something that can never be taken away regardless of what might follow directly on its heels. Playoffs can be brutal business. A quick loss can overshadow everything that was accomplished in a 162-game season. The win that says you get to keep playing is a milestone of its own. No matter the specter that looms in the Division Series to come, the moment can't be snatched from us and it shouldn't fall prey to our amnesiac instincts. Gil forbid the Mets didn't get very far in this postseason, I hoped the season that saw them come so far so fast after waiting so long wouldn't get lost in any recriminatory shuffle.

Coming into 2015, our team had poured champagne on itself only sixteen times in its history, including seven instances when the motivation for a bubbly bath came from making it to the playoffs. The next pour, the one just aching to be uncorked in Cincinnati during the last weekend of September, was going to be sweet. I hoped the taste would translate over TV and linger in the Mets fan memory. As the droughts following the final celebrations of 1973 (thirteen years), 1988 (eleven), 2000 (six) and 2006 (nine and thankfully no more) proved all too well, you never know when the next bottle will be opened.

* * *

I also found myself with a soft spot for those who were Mets not so long ago but not Mets any longer, the Mets who kept the uniforms filled and the dugout occupied and our hopes modestly aloft when there wasn't a drop of champagne to be spilled. As the clinching drew near, I thought about the Mets who never played on one of our teams that as much as contended for a playoff spot, the Mets who never saw even an 81st win.

Between 2009 and 2014, there were, by my reckoning, 115 Mets players who hadn't been part of the last contending Mets of 2008 and wouldn't be listed among the soon-to-be champion Mets of 2015.

The ones you pinned your intermittent aspirations on: Ike Davis. Josh Thole. Fernando Martinez.

The ones who had to travel elsewhere to approach the postseason: R. A. Dickey. Justin Turner. Collin McHugh. Both Chris Youngs.

The ones you linked by mellifluousness: Josh Stinson. Chris Schwinden. Josh Satin.

The ones you lumped by circumstance: Aaron Harang. Daisuke Matsuzaka (journeymen starters on the long journey to the end of 2013).

The ones who may have been the salt of the earth, but their existence struck you as vaguely fictional: Taylor Teagarden. Tobi Stoner. Lance Broadway. Jack Egbert.

The ones on whom you were just vague: Mike O'Connor. Justin Hampson. Elvin Ramirez. Or was it Ramon Ramirez? (No, actually, it was both.)

The ones who soaked up innings because somebody had to: Pat Misch. Elmer Dessens. Brandon Lyon. Raul Valdes.

The ones who hit because nobody better was available: Jesus Feliciano. Chris Carter. Jason Pridie. Mike Hessman on hiatus from being the minor league home run king.

Collin Cowgill, who hit a grand slam on Opening Day 2013 and slid downhill from there. Jordany Valdespin, who had a penchant for pinch homers and teammate alienation. Hisanori Takahashi, who was a one-year wonder in the rotation and relief. Shaun Marcum, who thought our beloved TV announcers didn't know what they were talking about when they correctly called attention to his shortcomings. Omar Quintanilla, who regularly leapt for line drives he had no hope of catching. Jeremy Hefner, who did not bounce back from Tommy John surgery. Mike Baxter, who preserved Johan Santana's no-hitter at the expense of his own left shoulder. Rob Johnson, who pitched an inning as a catcher. Gary Sheffield, who dropped by to slug his 500th homer. Omir Santos, who drove Jonathan Papelbon over the Green Monster. D. J. Carrasco, who balked home a walk-off run in Atlanta.

Tim Byrdak and Marlon Byrd and Scott Hairston and Zach Lutz and Dana Eveland and Greg Burke and Emil Brown and Vinny Rottino and Jose Valverde and . . .

They and dozens of others were the Mets we rooted for before better Mets, or at least a better mix of Mets, came along. All had moved on from our midst. Some were retired from baseball. Some were trying their best not to be. A few were on the verge of taking part in the very same playoffs the Mets were headed toward.

None would be eligible for World Series rings or shares in Flushing. None would be anywhere within spritzing distance of the joyous Mets clubhouse when Champagne Celebration No. 17 took flight. The least somebody could do was think about them for a minute. So I did.

Then I watched the present-day Mets, about whom I'd been thinking all year, close in on a clinching.

* * *

On Thursday night, September 24, Steven Matz wasn't as sharp as he'd been in his previous outing against the Yankees, giving up three runs and 10 hits in five-and-two-thirds innings. Erik Goeddel bailed him out of further trouble and positioned himself, the way relievers who face one batter will, as the pitcher of record when Daniel Murphy (triple), Yoenis Cespedes (single), and Lucas Duda (double) each drove in a run in the visitors' seventh.

The Mets took a 6–3 lead and went on to win, 6–4. The Nationals lost at home to the Orioles. The magic number was down to three.

On Friday night September 25, Noah Syndergaard keyed his own go-ahead run, just like in the offense-free days of May and June. Noah's RBI single in the second didn't have to stand alone, however. Duda blasted a three-run homer in the third, Curtis Granderson doubled in additional insurance in the seventh and the cushion became a rout once Murphy singled and Duda walloped another three-run job. Thor was able to concentrate on pitching, striking out 11 over seven-and-two-thirds. The Mets were 12–5 winners. In our nation's capital, the Phillies pounced on the Nats. The magic number was down to one.

One Met win or one National loss would confirm the New York Mets as champions of the National League Eastern Division for 2015.

A Met win was preferred. Who would have thought we'd get to make a choice?

* * *

On Saturday afternoon, September 26, in the top of the first inning, David Wright walked with one out against Reds starter John Lamb. Murphy singled with two out. Travis d'Arnaud walked. The bases were loaded for Duda, who was spending the entire weekend parked in an unloading zone. Duda swung and led Lamb to the slaughter. It was another Lucas long ball, a grand slam that staked Matt Harvey—in one of his select September appearances—to a 4–0 lead. Granderson would add to it with a solo homer in the second. Harvey permitted two runs in the bottom of that inning, but Michael Cuddyer got them both back for him ASAP, doubling home a pair in the third.

The Mets led, 7–2. The Nationals game was flying by. After nearly six months, this was no time to start rooting for Washington, but aesthetics demanded a little rain or a surfeit of replay reviews in their game. As long as we had the option of how we could clinch, we preferred the proactive model. We wanted the Mets to officially win the division before the Nationals could lose it.

The Nationals took a 1–0 lead in the sixth at Nationals Park. The Phillies tied it up in the eighth. Good. Stay busy, both of you. The Mets game was being a wee bit pokey. There wasn't much drama left from a scoreboard perspective, but there two moments to relish as we awaited the big one.

* * *

Harvey did not limit his exposure nor have it limited for him. In his previous start, versus the Yankees, he was brilliant—one hit, one walk, no runs—but exited after five because, well, Matt can't be expected to pitch a sixth inning . . . can he? The Mets' pen got lit up as soon he left that night, casting his outing in an ambiguous light. Sure he pitched great, but was he really going to allow himself to be pulled after five in the playoffs just because his agent insisted? If he was healthy (and nobody suggested he wasn't), where did the team fit into Matt's priorities?

In Cincinnati, the vibe veered to Boras Be Damned. Harvey asked Terry Collins for the ball for the seventh and the skipper gave it to him. He retired two of his last three Reds and left after six-and-two-thirds, still up by five runs. It wasn't his most scintillating outing (he scattered nine hits), but it was his most encouraging. After all the yammering over how little he might pitch in the fall, autumn had arrived and Harvey appeared prepared to embrace its challenges.

In the top of the ninth, the five-run Met lead grew to eight when Kelly Johnson singled, Granderson singled and a ball jumped off the bat of the Captain. It traveled well over the fence in left-center to make the score 10–2 and elevate the already Amazin' occasion to a status approaching consecrated. In another season, a Wright home run in a pending blowout victory would have been worth a golf clap. In this season, when there had been only five home runs from David and would be only 38 games played—the bulk of them with a back burdened by spinal stenosis—this clout took the emotional cake.

"Perhaps as fitting a hit as the Mets have had all year," pronounced Howie Rose at the tail end of a "magical afternoon in a fairy tale season."

* * *

Nothing was decided in Washington, where extra innings for two NL East also-rans became the order of the day. The Nationals had surely sunk into some sort of post-contention purgatory, punctuated the next day when the devil over Papelbon's shoulder goaded him into choking Bryce Harper . . . the team's franchise player . . . in the team's dugout . . . surrounded by teammates . . . while the game was going on . . . in full view of television cameras. With no danger the division would be clinched via any hand but their own, the Mets went to the bottom of the ninth intending to affix an 'x' next to their name in the standings for the first time since 2006.

Jeurys Familia came on to protect the eight-run lead. When you've waited nine years, the final three outs transcend the notion of a save situation. Familia got two quick outs. Then he gave up two quick hits. Then he faced Jay Bruce, who was briefly a Met trade target but whose fate it was to be folded into a Met trivia answer.

Name the eight men who made the final out in games that sent the Mets to the playoffs.

Joe Torre, September 24, 1969.

Glenn Beckert, October 1, 1973.

Chico Walker, September 17, 1986.

Lance Parrish, September 22, 1988.

Dmitri Young, October 4, 1999.

Keith Lockhart, September 27, 2000.

Josh Willingham, September 18, 2006.

Jay Bruce, September 26, 2015.

* * *

It was a swinging strike on an 0-2 count. As the ball settled in d'Arnaud's glove, you could put in the books the Mets' 88th win in 155 games and a nine-game lead with seven to go.

Strike three was caught, but the Mets couldn't be. They were champs.

"Tears of joy for the 2015 New York Mets!" Gary Cohen proclaimed in a callback to the season's pivot point, Wilmer Flores jubilantly homering forty-eight or so hours after visibly weeping. Now the liquid that would be in everybody's eyes would flow from fancy bottles. What didn't sting pupils (or land on wisely provided goggles) would go down easy. The Mets— Wright, Familia, Harvey, Granderson, Duda, all of them—drank it in. The fans who followed them to Cincinnati would have their symbolic sip when the players emerged from the clubhouse to thank them for being as much a part of the journey as fans could be. Those of us who watched on TV guzzled the good feelings in copious amounts.

Our team was a champion. Our time was now.

SETTING THE STAGE

The Mets fielded one of those classic day-after lineups in the game that followed their clinching and whupped up on the Reds anyway, 8–1. It was their eighth series sweep in the previous two months and an indication of how efficient they could be when presented with a less than imposing opponent. The Mets went 7–0 versus last-place Cincinnati in 2015 to go with 7–0 against last-place Colorado. It certainly balanced out the 0–13 mark they posted against potential playoff opponents from Pittsburgh and Chicago.

The September 27 win over the Reds was significant unto itself in that Sandy Alderson intimated in early February that the Mets should attain 89 wins. They'd won 79 in 2014 and he said he thought they were capable of winning 10 more in the year ahead. 79 + 10 did indeed equal 89. After 2014's Nostradamus misfire—when Alderson didn't precisely predict 90 wins, even though it came out that way in the papers—it was satisfying to see the Mets had lived up to a high expectation.

Achieving 90 wins in 2015 looked good and round as numbers went and it appeared to be easily within reach with six games remaining, but as the final week of the regular season began, the Mets forgot that they didn't know how to lose. They suffered a gloomy sweep in Philadelphia and crossed their fingers that Yoenis Cespedes didn't suffer any damage from the contusion he incurred when hit by a Justin De Fratus pitch. Cespedes was deemed physically fit, but the Mets bats looked dead tired. Their somnambulant state filtered into the final weekend at Citi Field. In the day-night doubleheader of Saturday, October 3 (the night before was a rainout, the only one the Mets encountered all year, not counting that suspended game in late June), they collected only five hits in the two games: five in the day portion, none at night.

* * *

That's right, the Mets were no-hit. Again. This time the pitcher who altogether stymied them was Max Scherzer. At last the Nationals were figuring out how to beat the Mets.

There were no divisional stakes between the Nats and Mets any longer, but home field advantage in the upcoming Division Series between the Dodgers and Mets had been up in the air throughout the week. If the Mets had shown any offense, they'd host a potential fifth game at Citi Field. As it happened, their lifelessness cost them that possible edge. We now knew they'd open their first playoff series in nine years at Dodger Stadium and not come home until Game Three.

Hence, the last time we'd see the Mets for a while was going to be Sunday October 4, a.k.a. Closing Day. Obviously Citi Field would be reopening for business in the NLDS, but the regular-season finale nevertheless managed to blend its annual dollop of melancholy with the sense of anticipation of what the playoffs would bring. Plus there was still that elusive 90th win and the desire to not watch our division champs limp west shrouded in a six-game losing streak.

On what seemed like the first sunny day in ages, the Mets did what teams headed for the playoffs do: they tuned up. Jacob deGrom pitched four scoreless innings. He was followed to the mound by six pitchers, five of whom would join him on the postseason roster, two of whom had been in the rotation until very recently. Terry Collins had decided to go young against the Dodgers. His kids—deGrom, Noah Syndergaard, Matt Harvey, and Steven Matz (if Matz wasn't sidelined by a sore back)—would go in Games One through Four. His vets, Bartolo Colon and Jon Niese, were now relievers.

Colon and Niese got their work in versus the Nats; Niese gave up the first hit the staff allowed, with two out in the seventh. Addison Reed and Tyler Clippard, the designated seventh- and eighth-inning men, also threw. The bullpen was fortified for October even if it never exactly felt settled.

* * *

The Mets weren't giving up hits but they weren't generating many, either. The game stayed scoreless into the bottom of the eighth, until Curtis Granderson, the only position player who maintained good health and a spot in the lineup virtually every day of the regular season, belted a home run off Blake Treinen. That made it 1–0, Mets. Jeurys Familia, despite giving up a two-out double to Bryce Harper, secured the 27th out, giving him a share of the team record for saves (43, held jointly with Armando Benitez) and the team its 90th win. The 90–72 Mets wound up taking the division by seven games.

We 41,631 who raised Citi Field's attendance for the season to 2,569,753, the ballpark's best since its inaugural year of 2009, appreciated the numbers. And the gestures. Closing Days are sanctified by their gestures as much as their statistics. The gestures were even better than the 2016 magnetic schedules they gave everybody.

Connoisseurs of Closing Day know the day isn't done just because the game is over. If the Mets win, you stand and you applaud and you wait to see what will happen next. It used to be the best you could hope for was a montage of video clips from the season we'd just persevered through and maybe a cluster of Mets gathering outside their dugout and tossing a few wristbands and well wishes to the fans nearby.

This time we got something more. We got something I'd never previously seen a Mets team give.

* * *

The Mets, every wonderful one of 'em, transformed themselves into a human highlight film. They came out en masse and they waved, but they didn't stop there. They jogged the circumference of the field. They greeted every segment of the stadium. It would have been easy enough to make a beeline to the monochromatically clothed, volubly unmatched 7 Line Army out in center and then a beeline right back into their clubhouse. The 7 Liners are the most visible cluster of fans at any game they hold down seats and they can't help but attract the most attention.

These Mets, though, symbolically recognized *everybody* who came out to recognize them. It was such a simple gesture, yet it ran so deep. The manager circled the field. The Captain circled the field. Everybody, whether they figured to make the postseason roster or not, circled the field. The effect was electric. It was like they, the players, knew who we were and how much we care; like they knew we show up to see them across 81 home games plus however many times some of us hit the road to lend them support. All we ask for in the course of the season is that the hitters pile up runs and the pitchers allow almost none. We wouldn't have thought of asking for this.

Yet they thought to give it to us. It was a splendid moment, topped only when David Wright grabbed a microphone to share a few gratitude-laced sentiments before encouraging all of us, "Let's go beat LA"

Yes, we agreed aloud. Let's.

HOW WE GOT PAST LA

ANIMAL PLANET

G ame 162 was Sunday. Game One wouldn't be until Friday. The waiting was interminable. Distractions were welcome.

We had the distraction provided by the determination of who would
take the final spots on the roster. Forty-nine different players saw action
as Mets in 2015, including 39 in a particularly expansive September. The
postseason allowed only 25. The only doubt remained along the margins.

Eric Campbell covered third base in the middle of summer. Logan Verrett was a valuable swing man. Anthony Recker had been part of the Mets'
bench since 2013. Bobby Parnell, the bullpen's elder statesman, went all
the way back to 2008. Each was dispatched to Port St. Lucie to work out
and stay ready. They'd never be heard from again in 2015. Nor would we
see any more of Carlos Torres, whose constancy on the 25-man roster was
derailed by his strained calf in September. He never went on the DL, but he
wasn't invited to the postseason party.

Neither was Eric Young Jr., who had established one of the bizarre
records in franchise history. Young was the semi-regular left fielder in 2013
and 2014 before signing with Atlanta in the last offseason. Things didn't go
well with the Braves and eventually the Mets signed him to a minor league
deal with the idea that he'd provide pinch-running flexibility in the postseason. Terry Collins deployed him very specifically in September and the
experiment yielded a singular season line. EYJ came to bat nine times, was
hit by a pitch once, made out in his eight other appearances . . . yet scored
nine runs. Young's productivity broke a 36-year-old mark that belonged
to the immortal Sergio Ferrer. In 1979, Ferrer, the utilityest of utility

infielders, scored seven runs despite going 0-for-7 on the season. "Little Sergio," as broadcaster Steve Albert called him, was robbed of his only base hit by future Met Ray Knight at the end of the Mets' first-ever 10-run inning that June.

If I haven't forgotten that by now, I'm probably never going to.

EYJ's ability to accentuate the positive (no, he couldn't hit, but runs scored are the name of the game—right?) made him a hero to those of us who revel in statistical quirks, but it must not have impressed Terry Collins or Sandy Alderson. He was exiled to the taxi squad with Soup and the gang.

The Met who was projected to bring a significant right-handed bat off the bench would also be absent from the postseason roster, at least for the first round. Juan Uribe injured his chest while diving for a ground ball during the last Subway Series and aggravated it while pinch-hitting in Cincinnati. Despite representing experience, leadership and pinch-hitting power, he wouldn't be activated. His unavailability cleared a path for Kirk Nieuwenhuis, a speedy lefty hitter who was also something of a good-luck charm.

The final decision also came down to an injury. Steven Matz's back hadn't been quite right since he woke up feeling stiff during the last week of the season. Matz's status would affect whether a) Bartolo Colon returned to the rotation and b) Sean Gilmartin made the Dodger series at all. Gilmartin had to remain on the roster the entire regular season in deference to his Rule 5 situation. Ironically, once Matz was declared healthy, Gilmartin was instructed to step aside.

* * *

Ladies and gentlemen, the first Mets postseason roster since October 19, 2006:

CATCHERS: Travis d'Arnaud, Kevin Plawecki

INFIELDERS: Lucas Duda, Daniel Murphy, Wilmer Flores, David Wright, Kelly Johnson, Ruben Tejada

OUTFIELDERS: Michael Cuddyer, Yoenis Cespedes, Curtis Granderson, Michael Conforto, Juan Lagares, Nieuwenhuis

STARTING PITCHERS: Jacob deGrom, Noah Syndergaard, Matt Harvey, Matz

RELIEF PITCHERS: Colon, Jon Niese, Erik Goeddel, Hansel Robles, Addison Reed, Tyler Clippard, Jeurys Familia

So the Mets knew who they were bringing to Los Angeles. And goodness knows they knew who they'd be facing once they got there. "Those two animals" is how Collins, in his increasingly entertaining stream of consciousness, described Clayton Kershaw and Zack Greinke. By labeling them animals, Terry was basically admitting they loomed as superhuman.

* * *

Game One starter Kershaw in 2015: 16–7, 2.13 ERA, 301 SO & 42 BB in 232 2/3 IP.

Game Two starter Greinke in 2015: 19–3, 1.66 ERA, 200 SO & 40 BB in 222 2/3 IP.

Animal, vegetable, mineral . . . classify them as you will, those guys were going to be tough, especially on that legendary Dodger Stadium mound, particularly if MLB stuck us with a start time that added shadows to the Chavez Ravine pitchscape. The Mets lucked out in that their games wouldn't begin until 9:45 on Friday night, October 9 and 9:07 Saturday night, October 10. Blessed with one fewer impediment, Mets fans turned on a dime from fretting over shadows to moaning that the games were starting too late, how would we ever stay up?

This wasn't going to be a problem for me. I'd been lying awake at night since September 2007 wondering if we'd ever make the playoffs again.

We needed more distractions. For an hour or two, we had the Case of the Missing Harvey. Matt showed up late for a workout at Citi Field on Tuesday, October 6. His explanations were a bit murky, but he seemed to be alive, well, and preparing to pitch. Everybody moved on.

* * *

We had actual baseball from other precincts to distract us next. The first postseason game of 2015 was played Tuesday night at Yankee Stadium. Carlos Gomez and the upstart Astros were taking on the high and mighty Bronx Bombers in the American League Wild Card game. Well, they couldn't have been too high and mighty if they were reduced to scrounging about in the win-or-leave contraption baseball invented in 2012. The Yankees had been surpassed by the rampaging Blue Jays in August and had to settle for wild card scraps.

And that was all they got in the end. Dallas Keuchel and three Houston relievers shut them out on three hits and the Yankees' October was over nine innings after it began. Whatever characteristic *Sheadenfreude* we treated ourselves to was spiked with the delicious knowledge that we'd have New York to ourselves for the rest of the postseason. If nothing else, at least we'd get three games of solitary spotlight. Honestly, it wasn't that big a deal, considering the Yankees losing to the Astros wasn't going to help the Mets beat the Dodgers.

But after finishing with a simultaneous better record *and* higher standing than our local American League counterparts for the first time since 1990, this was a pleasant palate-cleanser. The opportunity to make New York an overwhelmingly Mets town, if just for the month ahead, belonged to the Mets. Win and there'd be no other team on most people's lips.

Call it the spoils of postseason. It wasn't the goal, but it sure would be nice.

Wednesday night, October 7, brought the National League Wild Card game, pitting the 98-win Pirates against the 97-win Cubs, each of whom finished behind the 100-win Cardinals in the NL Central. Strange that one of them was about to follow the Yankees home while the 92-win Dodgers and 90-win Mets (not to mention the 86-win Astros) were guaranteed to play in a Division Series. With the postseason configured to award division-winners, something like this was bound to happen one of these years. In the fourth year of the present format, it happened to the 98-win Pirates, who were thoroughly thwarted by Jake Arietta and the Cubs. Chicago would play St. Louis. Houston was going up against Kansas City. Toronto had to take on Texas. All of those series would have at least one game played before the Mets and Dodgers *finally* got down to business.

The Mets. The Dodgers. The playoffs. The last time somebody threw a pitch at a Met in this kind of scenario, it was Adam Wainwright breaking off an ungodly curveball that Carlos Beltran watched until it landed as strike three in the mitt of Yadier Molina. We lived with that as our lasting image of October every day for the rest of 2006, then through all of 2007 and onward until a moment could come along and replace it as Most Recent Pitch in a Met Playoff Game.

Granderson touched off a new postseason chapter shortly after 6:45 p.m. Pacific Daylight Time—ten days shy of nine years later—by swinging at the first pitch Kershaw threw. He lined it to right, where it was caught by Andre Ethier. It was an out, but it was something.

It was something else. The Mets were playing playoff baseball.

* * *

The Dodger aces may have ruled the animal kingdom, but our guys were no pussycats. What was it David Ortiz said in August after a weekend's exposure to the arms of Flushing? "The Mets, with that pitching staff, they're not too far away from walking into the money." What Big Papi said, the rest of the baseball-watching world was about to find out for themselves.

DeGrom. Syndergaard. Harvey. Matz. Those things they did with a baseball were well-known to us, maybe not yet to everybody else. Their hours spent in the shadows of the likes of Kershaw and Greinke were about to end.

It was time for America to meet the wonders.

First up, Jacob deGrom, resembling the All-Star who dazzled the American League three months earlier. That night he struck out three batters on ten pitches. On this night, he came out firing in the same vein. Clayton Kershaw fanned two Mets in the top of the first? DeGrom answered by whiffing three Dodgers.

It was on. Two pitchers of impeccable credentials were dueling as darkness descended on the San Gabriel Mountains. Dodger Stadium was planted in as beautiful a setting as any in the big leagues. The pitching displayed there that Friday night was just as enchanting.

Modest threats materialized, then evaporated. There was no scoring for three innings. Kershaw had struck out six Mets, deGrom seven Dodgers.

Daniel Murphy stepped in to lead off the top of the fourth and, for not the last time in the month of October, put his imprint on the postseason.

Literally. Murphy got hold of a Kershaw delivery and smoked it over the right field fence. He hit it so hard that when the ball was recovered, the name DANIEL was visibly emblazoned backwards into the ol' cowhide. It came from his bat. The exit velocity of Murph's home run was measured at 105 MPH . . . and six capital letters.

Kershaw was so shaken that he proceeded to strike out Travis d'Arnaud looking and Lucas Duda swinging before retiring Michael Cuddyer on fly ball to center. The reigning NL MVP had run into problems in the post-season before. Except for running into Murphy's bat, he wasn't having too much difficulty with the 2015 Met lineup.

But he was losing and deGrom made sure he'd continue to. Justin Turner led off the home fourth with his second hit of the night—Justin was apparently still wreaking vengeance on the Mets for unceremoniously non-tendering him two winters earlier—but Jacob escaped unscathed. The fifth brought more soft breezes to Chavez Ravine; three Met K's in the top of the inning (two swinging), two Dodger K's in the bottom (both swinging). The respective sides were retired in order in the sixth.

* * *

It was still 1–0 when Kershaw lost a bit of control to open the seventh. He walked Duda. Cuddyer grounded to third, which moved Lucas up a base. Tejada walked on a full count. DeGrom bunted both of them over. Curtis Granderson walked on a 3-2 pitch to put a Met on each base.

Don Mattingly removed Kershaw after four walks, four hits, the one run, and 11 strikeouts, 113 pitches in all. His choice to replace him was . . . well, it wasn't Clayton Kershaw. The Mets had gotten him out of the game and held the lead. That was half the battle.

The other half was making something out of this sudden sacks-packed bounty versus Dodgers reliever Pedro Baez. David Wright was up next. The same David Wright who, like those of us watching on TBS, had been waiting a very long time for this first Met playoff game since October 19, 2006, let alone the first Met playoff win since October 18, 2006. The first year TBS aired a portion of the MLB postseason was 2007. To alert baseball fans everywhere, the cable channel prepared advertising that September which featured players it was certain would be part of its coverage. Showing up in brochures and on billboards was the Mets' third baseman, then twenty-four. Now thirty-two, David was at last making his TBS October debut.

The wait was fully shed from Wright's shoulders when he stroked Baez's 3-2 pitch into center field. Duda and Tejada scored to put the Mets up, 3–0. Thus fortified, deGrom returned to the mound in the bottom of the seventh and set down the Dodgers in order, striking out Joc Pederson and pinch-hitter Chase Utley for emphasis.

DeGrom had gone as far as Terry Collins was inclined to let him, but what a path he blazed: 7 IP, 5 H, 1 BB, 13 SO (plus impressive impishness; he furtively lowered the height of Murphy's chair during the postgame press conference while Daniel was answering a question). His strikeout total was the stuff of franchise legend. Only Tom Seaver and Doc Gooden had fanned double-digit batters in a Mets postseason game; only Tom had turned it up to 13.

Select company for Jacob. In the present, he'd be joined in the box score by Tyler Clippard, who gave back one run in two-thirds of the eighth inning, and Jeurys Familia, who'd record four outs over the eighth and ninth to nail down the Game One victory, a 3–1 Mets triumph.

The Mets had taken their first step into the money. The second wouldn't be quite so simple. It never is when somebody goes out of his way to violently get in your way.

SLIDE INTO MADNESS

Keith Hernandez often directs his more tutorial observations to "all you kids out there." Well, for all the kids who were staying up late on Saturday night, October 10, to watch Game Two, there was a new lesson: You can now play baseball any way you like. The rules don't apply. Just slam into middle infielders at will. You don't even need to be on your way to second base. You do this, and your team shall be handsomely rewarded.

That was my interpretation after a playoff game that roving bands of baserunners and umpires conspired to take away from the New York Mets. The Mets might have given Saturday's contest away themselves, but the dirtiest of Dodgers and his de facto co-conspirators couldn't depend on that to happen.

Just my unbiased take.

* * *

In the seventh inning of Game Two—with the Mets leading the Dodgers, 2–1—Chase Utley slid into and did physical damage unto Ruben Tejada without a base being close to his body or his thoughts. The slide transpired in the midst of Tejada attempting to turn a double play. It probably wouldn't have been a double play on its own merit even had Utley not essentially tackled Tejada. It might not have technically been a single play, given that Tejada did not step on the bag. Second base umpire Chris Guccione called Utley out initially because umpires make mistakes. Replay review exists to correct them. Replay showed that Tejada, in taking an imperfect feed from Daniel Murphy on Howie Kendrick's sharp one-out chopper up the middle amid what had been a first-and-third situation, missed the bag by a hair before attempting to set and fire to first.

On the other hand, it could have been called a neighborhood play, in which case Guccione wasn't off base, even though Tejada was. A neighborhood play is the one play on the diamond for which everybody opts to overlook the basic rule about a fielder's foot needing to touch a base in order to record a putout. It is too dangerous, all quietly concur, to penalize a shortstop or second baseman for protecting his life and limb from an onrushing baserunner. *We all know the runner's gonna be out, let's just call him out.* That's the gentlemen's agreement.

Chase Utley is no gentleman, which is his business, except when his business becomes the maiming of Ruben Tejada or any middle infielder he essentially attacks while not much attempting to reach second base. Utley said he wasn't trying to break Tejada's leg, even though that's exactly what he did. He said he was trying to break up a double play. That's fine. Except—and we learned this eight years before when Marlon Anderson was our baserunner trying to do something sort of similar—you can't break up double plays without making second base your reasonably realistic destination.

* * *

Utley slid exceedingly late into Tejada with zero intention of sliding into second. In fact, wherever Tejada's foot had been an instant earlier, Utley never reached second, not even as a matter of follow-through. He broke apart a double play and, incidentally, the fielder's fibula. Utley may very well have wished no harm come from his action, but he did act and there was harm. That's cause enough to declare an inning-ending double play. It was a double play in 2007 when Anderson was ruled to have slid away from second base in order to interfere with an opposition fielder (Utley's then-Phillis teammate Tad Iguchi) and it should have been a double play in Game Two.

Instead, because baseball's officiating infrastructure is the envy of Swiss cheese producers the world over, somehow Utley—who never touched second; who never really tried to touch second; who sacked Tejada as if Ruben were scrambling behind the line of scrimmage—was told he was not out. He was allowed to stand at second base, a spot that was never on his itinerary. Meanwhile, the runner on third, Kiké Hernandez, had scored to make it 2–2 and Kendrick was on first. There was still only one out and nothing good was going to come of any of this.

Nothing did. Noah Syndergaard's breathtaking six-and-a-third innings of nine-strikeout starting pitching went for naught. Solo home runs blasted off Zack Greinke in the second inning by Yoenis Cespedes and Michael Conforto (the latter a laser that smacked the right field foul pole) were matched and surpassed when Adrian Gonzalez lashed a two-run double to right off Addison Reed one out after Utley's literal takeout of Tejada. Justin Turner followed by continuing to dish out more cold revenge on his former team, this time in the form of an RBI double.

Worth mentioning, too: the Mets couldn't touch Greinke after their solo shots in the second. Two runs in seven frames are better than most teams did against the NL Cy Young candidate in any given game in 2015, but it wasn't enough to withstand Utley Gone Wild.

* * *

Some or all of the seventh-inning carnage inflicted on Syndergaard, Bartolo Colon (who threw the fateful pitch to Kendrick), and Reed could have been avoided had a valid judgment call been made that Utley slid dangerously and illegally. Deem it "hard-nosed" or brand it with some other charming euphemism, the inference that could be drawn from any angle is that Utley wasn't trying to reach second base. He wasn't coming close to second base. He went after Tejada. He didn't remotely disguise his real target.

How that was overlooked, I have no idea. Explanations so shaky they could have rumbled up from the San Andreas Fault were proffered later— MLB Secretary of Explaining Stuff Joe Torre was at a loss to delineate how a runner initially called out should have been tagged by a broken-legged fielder just in case he wasn't actually out—but they solved nothing . . . just as Met hitters didn't solve Greinke and two Dodger relievers . . . just as Reed didn't solve two of the three hitters he was tasked with retiring.

So the Mets lost the second game of the NLDS, 5–2, and they lost their shortstop. Since he first made the team as twenty-year-old in 2010, Tejada had proven himself an uncommonly resilient cat. The number of lives he'd had as a Met stalwart was displayed on the back of his jersey. Hell, No. 11 was getting clobbered on dubious slides by Chase Utley back when he was a rookie under Jerry Manuel. How many times had we dismissed Ruben's potential contributions only to find him back in the lineup, working counts, tiring pitchers, and subtly creating offense? How many times had we looked for another shortstop only to find us looking to good ol' Ruben to get us the out we needed? We finally wind up in the playoffs and who did we see starting ahead of folk hero Wilmer Flores?

We would miss Tejada on principle, and not just for the way he went down. He was one of ours and he should have been available to play a part in our finest hour. Make no mistake; we were still in the midst of that hour. Game Two was a blow—both the loss of the shortstop and the loss of the game—but we went to LA and beat one of the two great Dodger mounds-men. We left no worse than even.

Now it was back to New York, with two more aces up our sleeve for Game Three. One was Matt Harvey. The other, to my surprise, was Citi Field.

ECHOES OF SHEA

Let's not overlook the contributions of those listed in the NLDS Game Three box score. Curtis Granderson pounded a three-run double and drove in five altogether. Yoenis Cespedes catapulted a home run into the Left Field Landing. There were three RBIs from Travis d'Arnaud and three runs scored by Juan Lagares. Matt Harvey, usually the focus of any contest he pitches, unassumingly overcame a jagged second inning and gave his club five effective frames. By the time he left, the Mets were ahead, 10–3.

Whereas the Mets were able to follow up Jacob deGrom and Noah Syndergaard with Harvey, the Dodgers had no sequel remotely equivalent to Clayton Kershaw and Zack Greinke. The Mets lit up LA starter Brett Anderson and just about every reliever who came along in his wake. Game Three was a foregone conclusion early and often, its final logging in at 13–7 in the Mets' favor.

Hurrah for the Mets who made it happen. They deserve, oh, a good 99.99 percent of the credit for the resounding victory that pushed the club within one game of clinching the best-of-five National League Division Series. Seriously, we couldn't have done it without them.

Yet when I look back at Game Three, the details of the action itself will probably always take a back seat to how Citi Field came out of its shell once and for all and emerged as the full-throated home of the New York Mets.

It took only seven years.

* * *

One can quibble over whether buildings can be imbued with human characteristics, but if we grant the notion validity, then Citi Field could have been described as aloof, muted, and perhaps a bit of a wallflower from the April evening it opened in 2009. It made little more noise than it had to until it had unambiguous reason to shout its head off on July 31, 2015, the night Wilmer Flores definitively turned our collective frown upside down.

One more rite of passage—a final test of legitimacy—awaited the seven-year-old ballpark on Monday night, October 12. It had to speak up in a postseason conversation. It had to create a din and make itself heard over it. It had to, no matter the pains its architects went to ensure it would in no way resemble its predecessor, carry on like Shea Stadium.

For Game Three, it did. And so did we.

The pregame introductions set the tone for Citi Field's inaugural play-off engagement. First home games of postseason series bring the pomp and the circumstance and enormous opportunity for self-expression. Almost every one of us among the 44,276 in the seats and taking up standing room opted to vocally share one opinion above all others.

And it wasn't in favor of Chase Utley.

Anybody whose memory stretched back at least to John Rocker in 1999 let alone Pete Rose in 1973 knew that Shea Stadium villains always heard from their detractors come October. Nobody was endorsing the flying water and whiskey bottles of yore (and none was flung as far as I could tell), but nowhere on the fine print on the backs of the tickets did it say we couldn't bring our enmity to bear. So we did.

You wouldn't believe how many different ways there were to tell Utley how much he sucked during the introductions and throughout the game. The disgraced baserunner could have saved himself an earful by accepting the two-game suspension MLB handed down for his heinous slide in Los Angeles, but Utley appealed the decision and thus made himself eligible for use in Games Three and Four. Don Mattingly resisted the temptation.

* * *

Lest we be thought of as overwhelmingly negative, we the 44,276 strong of Citi Field (give or take a few wayward souls dressed in Dodger blue) lent as much support to the home team as we spewed animus on the visitors. We cheered every Met player, every Met coach and every Met massage therapist and bullpen catcher. Matt Reynolds, the emergency call-up backup shortstop who had never set official foot on a major league diamond, was treated as warmly as the fellas who did the heavy lifting all season. We'd waited so long for a team to shower affection upon that we didn't stop all night. My neighbors in Section 131 probably set a record for most LET'S GO METSes before the Mets ever came to bat.

The roar of roars was reserved for the Met who wouldn't be playing. In a shrewd slice of stagecraft, the most beloved player of all was introduced last. Limping out with the aid of a Mets-logoed cane, it was Ruben Tejada, still in one piece, still one of ours.

We went nuts. Not that we had far to go to get there. I can't stress enough what it was like to let loose after nine years without playoffs, wave those silly orange towels they handed you at the gate and christen Citi Field as a postseason venue. Through more than 200 regular-season games attended there, I'd wondered if a structure that seemed to be more about brand synergy than baseball soul could rise to an occasion like this.

Consider Citi Field risen. In the moments after Cespedes's bomb, I swear I felt the left field stands vibrate. I thought I'd never feel anything like that again after they tore down Shea.

I stood corrected.

* * *

But, y'know, we and our ballpark can't take more than 00.01 percent of the credit for winning Game Three. And, honestly, if we were so great, why couldn't we lift the Mets to a series victory in Game Four?

Oh right, Kershaw. The Dodgers started him on short rest on Tuesday, October 13, and he was as vintage Kershaw as he needed to be, going seven and giving up only three hits. One of them was a home run to Daniel Murphy, the second the ace of aces surrendered to the second baseman in the series, but no other Met meaningfully dented his armor. Steven Matz, meanwhile, was trying to do nothing more than clinch a postseason series for his childhood team in the seventh start of his injury-pocked career. He wasn't terrible, but—although he had been compared favorably to his opponent in terms of potential—he was not yet a match for Kershaw at his best. Despite our sincerest and loudest urgings, L.A. beat us, 3–1, and sent the series back to Dodger Stadium tied at two games apiece. The whole shebang would be decided on the West Coast.

Chase Utley sucked there, too, even if nobody was likely to chant it at high volumes.

BETTER MET THAN NEVER

It's a small detail from a big night, no more than a leaf on a tree in the forest of delight that emanated from Chavez Ravine Thursday night, October 15, as the New York Mets defeated the Los Angeles Dodgers, 3–2, to advance to the National League Championship Series. But the detail tells us a little something. There were three balls hit by Dodger batters to Met pitchers. Each was handled cleanly and converted into one or more outs. One of them went for a critical double play.

Those were four of 27 outs, all of them recorded because three different Met pitchers handled their position cleanly. SIMPLE TASK COMPLETED would read the non-existent headlines these plays could have theoretically inspired. Yet if you could recollect all the way back to 2014, mastering the mundane was an intermittent Met problem. Met pitchers made throws to bases adventures. In October of 2015, in the biggest game the Mets had played in nine years, it was all very routine. No ball was zipped down a line, none sailed into center.

A small detail, but a larger story. The Mets, who we would have had a hard time imagining playing for such high stakes one October earlier, got better at various aspects of their trade. Their pitchers got better at fielding their position. Their second baseman got better at thinking while in motion. Their manager got better at deciding who should be on the mound when.

The Mets got better and better as 2015 progressed and, as a result, they discovered themselves at the precipice of proving themselves the best in their league.

If you were a Mets fan, you might have expected it, but you probably didn't. For the longest time—in general and specifically within the cauldron of a hyperstressful deciding NLDS game—you more likely expected the worst, not so much from a reflexively fatalistic point of view, but just because the Mets of recent vintage had so rarely inspired confidence.

* * *

There didn't seem much cause to doubt them after Game Five at Dodger Stadium, even if they didn't exactly swamp their competition. Zack Greinke, the starting pitcher who had posted nearly the lowest regular-season ERA baseball had seen since the prime of young Doc Gooden, set most of them down in orderly procession well into the seventh inning. Unfortunately for him, he missed a Met.

Greinke absolutely dominated eight of the nine batters in the Met lineup. They were all but uniformly helpless against him. The exception early on: Daniel Murphy, who doubled home Curtis Granderson, who reached on a replay-reviewed infield single that somehow didn't award Chase Utley second, in the top of the first.

(Daniel Murphy—remember that name.)

Jacob deGrom didn't appear nearly as effective in his second start of the series. He gave back the 1–0 lead on four consecutive singles in the bottom of the first and found himself behind, 2–1. While Greinke took to mowing down Met after Met, Jacob kept dipping his toes into troubled waters. He left two on in the first, two on in the second, another on in the third. This wasn't the deGrom of Game One by a long shot.

Funny thing, though. As bad as Jacob looked and as much as the Dodgers filled up the basepaths, the score stayed stubbornly the same. LA wasn't cashing in, and deGrom wasn't going anywhere.

Greinke was gliding along into the fourth when the one Met who'd given him grief in the first third of the game came up again. It was Murphy, who produced a single. Greinke flied out Yoenis Cespedes and then, with his infield in a severe shift, walked Lucas Duda. Duda strolled to first. Murphy trotted to second.

Then he ran like nobody was watching. Because nobody was—no Dodger who could stop him, anyway. Murph correctly assessed that the

Duda shift, which transported so many fielders to the right side, would leave third base unoccupied.

Holy crap, you were entitled to think after so many seasons of Daniel running this way or that but not necessarily where he was supposed to go, *Murph just outsmarted an entire baseball team.*

Take that, Dodger Way!

Daniel stood on third with less than two out, which in a game of Greinke Versus the World is incredibly valuable. Now the Mets didn't need one of those base hits they couldn't get without Murph batting. All they needed was the right kind of out. Outs were a commodity they could manufacture like crazy against Greinke.

Travis d'Arnaud came through with a deep enough fly ball to Andre Ethier in right. It scored the heady Murphy with the tying run. The game wasn't necessarily won there, but it was kept from being lost. The Dodgers were punching themselves silly on offense. They threatened in the fourth and again in the fifth. DeGrom played rope-a-dope.

Still, it was difficult to picture a TKO of Greinke was in the offing. After Murphy stole third and a run, the Mets made five more outs in a row, taking them to the sixth, still tied. If only Murph could come up again and create more magic.

* * *

Murph came up again and created more magic. He homered to right on a 3-2 count. Taking on a pitcher who gave up one-and-two-thirds runs every nine innings during the regular season, Daniel accounted for three earned runs in three plate appearances.

And just like that, the Mets had a lead of 3–2, except there was no sense of "and just like that" to how they did it. Greinke did almost nothing wrong. He's as good a pitcher as there is, yet it was *his* line that read as distressingly ordinary. Sure, he struck out nine in six-and-two-thirds, and when he was Murphless, he was almost flawless, but you can't dominate only eight members of a nine-Met lineup.

DeGrom? He spent six innings in a slog. Even his one clean frame, the sixth, was nearly undone at its end when Greinke of all batters took him deep to right. Granderson caught that ball, though, and allowed Jacob to go to the dugout with the best so-so outing you'll ever thank your lucky stars for. Six hits, three walks, impending doom ... but only those two runs from the first inning. DeGrom left as a winning pitcher in every sense of the phrase.

He didn't outpitch Greinke. He outperformed him.

* * *

Concurrently, Terry Collins didn't panic. He could have pulled deGrom. A different manager might have looked at the odds in the second and done just that. This was lose-and-go-home territory. A fancy switch in which you replace a starting pitcher with another starting pitcher isn't merely fashionable in October. It is perfectly reasonable.

But it didn't happen, not until the seventh, when the several-times-warmed Noah Syndergaard was inserted in deGrom's place. Syndergaard was a rookie and a starter. He had never pitched relief in the majors. He was being told to partake of this exceedingly novel experience in the seventh inning of the fifth game of a five-game playoff series. Syndergaard's stuff ran rings around that of every pitcher Collins would normally use in a seventh inning, but this seventh inning was unlike all that had preceded them in 2015.

* * *

Which makes for a fascinating quandary: Do you use your best arm in an unfamiliar circumstance because it's the most important game of the year?

Answer A is yes, because it's the best arm you've got and the game is too important to screw around.

Answer is B is no, because it's an unfamiliar circumstance and the game is too important to screw around.

* * *

Collins, urged on by Dan Warthen, went with A. After a season when one of the most vexing subplots was "who will relieve in the seventh?" the manager chose someone who had never relieved in the seventh.

The best arm trumped the unfamiliar circumstance. Syndergaard was Syndergaard. Howie Kendrick tapped back to him; Corey Seager struck out; menacing Adrian Gonzalez walked; Justin Turner, who hit .526 in the NLDS, finally swung and missed.

Noah Syndergaard kept a 3–2 game 3–2. Then he was removed, which at first brush seemed absurd. You have this golden-armed, overpowering twenty-three-year-old who regularly throws 100 pitches and you sit him after 17?

You do. Terry got what he needed from Thor. He got the seventh. Syndergaard let it all hang out. Now it was time for . . .

Familia? Really?

Again, they're doing what they never do. When the Mets go to Jeurys in the eighth with two outs or one out it's treated as breaking news; you wait for Wolf Blitzer to interview a hologram of Hoyt Wilhelm. That's during the season. This is during the postseason. With well-rested bullpen professionals (not to mention almost all other starting hands on deck), you pick *now* to get a jump on closing the door? You ask Familia to get six outs when you *never* ask Familia to get six outs?

In another era, that was standard procedure. We who lived through that era love to point to it as proof of when firemen were firemen and relievers' arms were shipped directly from Akron, Ohio, rubber capital of North America. We assumed those days were gone forever.

We also thought we might never see the Mets in the playoffs again, yet here they were and here was Familia, on in the eighth. He treated the eighth like he treats most ninths—like they're no problem. He got his grounder back to the mound, then a liner to left, then—from classic Philadelphia thorn Jimmy Rollins—a hot grounder to first, smothered and snuffed out by Duda, who you would've thought was in there for his glove.

Despite all the State Farm and GEICO ads that inundated us every commercial break for six going on seven months, the Mets opted not to invest in a policy. They simply refused to insure their lead with an additional run. The offense had been Murphy and practically nothing but Murphy all night and, really, the entirety of the Dodger affair. There were flashes from others, primarily in Game Three's blowout, but several Mets chose the National League Division Series as a great time to fall into or stay in a slump. An enormous part of that was the presence of Kershaw and Greinke, but a few extra runs here and there would have been helpful. Except for Game Three, those runs never came.

With no cushion provided, Familia returned to the mound for the ninth with the same 3–2 lead that had been effect since the sixth. His first assignment was retiring the loathsome Utley, who shouldn't have been wearing any uniform by now unless it was an orange jumpsuit. Utley gave a ball a ride to right, but then the ball said, no thanks, I'll get out here, and fell into Granderson's glove. Met karma intact, Jeurys reared back and fanned A. J. Ellis, then Kendrick.

That, if you were scoring at home, was the 27th out. The Mets had won the game and the series, both by a final of 3–2.

* * *

The next sight you saw was their entire roster forming a ball of human Silly Putty. The next sound you heard was—for the 18th time in franchise history—the spritzing of champagne over everybody and everything orange, blue, and otherwise. The next thought we had was "tonight the Dodgers, Saturday the Cubs."

Then we thought a little more and tried to understand what we had just witnessed over five games, particularly inside the fifth game. The Mets did not let us down. The manager made more right moves than wrong ones. The pitchers threw almost exclusively extraordinary innings. The second baseman was, after a career that came off more as blooper reel than highlight film, a net Met positive. No Met screwed up enough to blow anything that couldn't be repaired.

Our New York Mets, who we were not used to seeing in the glowingest of lights and who we mopily assumed we wouldn't see at this time of year for many Octobers to come, were postseason winners. They had already won a division; now they had won a Division Series and were sanctioned to pursue a pennant. Four teams in all of the major leagues were still playing baseball. One of them was the Mets.

I'd say, "Imagine that," but it was really happening.

HOW WE GOT OURSELVES
A PENNANT

THE GREATEST SHOW
ON MURPH

Daniel Murphy did not singlehandedly win Game Five in Los Angeles for the Mets. I'm pretty sure I saw him use both hands.

As for the National League Championship Series against the Cubs, Murph may have simply levitated the whole thing. If there's another explanation for how one player—a pretty good player when all of his cylinders and synapses are firing, but not someone you'd peg as running on the fast track to Cooperstown—can take over an entire set of crucial games on behalf of his team, I'm open to evidence.

The NLCS belonged to Daniel Murphy. The rest of us were happy to be living somewhere near it.

While absorbed in Mets myopia during the first round, I didn't see much of the Cubs' conquest of the Cardinals, but I heard they were fairly efficient in taking down the Central Division champs in four games, one fewer than our guys needed to beat LA No team had been hotter coming into the postseason. The Cubs won 15 of their final 19 games, including their last eight in a row. The only teams in baseball with better records, the Pirates and Cardinals, fell victim to their blend of starters and sluggers. There was a lot of talent on that Chicago team ... the same team that took seven of seven games from the Mets in the regular season just past.

The Mets countered with Daniel Murphy. The Cubs couldn't possibly compete.

Never mind the trivia that was going around en route to Game One between the two old rivals, the bit about the curse baked into the Cubs' chances because there'd been a goat, a general manager (Johnny, our GM in 1969), a broadcaster (Bob, also ours) and a stadium (Jack, for Bob's San Diego sportswriting brother) each named Murphy, and something bad happened to the North Siders in their general vicinity at the absolute worst time. Daniel Murphy was luck enough all by himself in 2015. Good luck for the Mets. Good luck, anybody who tried to get him out.

Goat luck for the Cubs, but that was their problem.

* * *

On Saturday night, October 17, in Game One at chilly Citi Field—every bit as raucous as it had been for the Dodgers, save for having no Utley-like repository for jeers—Jon Lester presented a formidable opponent. He'd earned two World Series rings with Boston, solidified Chicago's rotation, beaten the Mets in May, and given up no runs to them in July.

But Lester had to face Murphy in October and that was pretty much that. The Cub starter got only ten pitches deep before Daniel took him over the right field wall for a 1–0 Mets lead. He had tagged Kershaw twice. Greinke once. Now Lester. Pretty impressive collection of baseball cards for Murph's locker.

Matt Harvey was perfect for four innings, a little less so in the fifth, when he hit leadoff man Anthony Rizzo for his first baserunner, then allowed a double to Starlin Castro for the Cubs' first run. An ill-advised decision by third base coach Gary Jones sent Castro toward home on Javier Baez's one-out single to center. Jones hadn't taken into account that Yoenis Cespedes would be throwing to Travis d'Arnaud. Castro was out easily and Harvey eased out of the fifth.

Nobody could have guessed then, but that represented the Cubs' best chance to take a lead . . . in the entire series.

The Mets pounced in their fashion in the bottom of the fifth. Wilmer Flores and Juan Lagares singled in succession with one out. Harvey's bunt was only partly useful, as it forced Flores at third. It wasn't a total loss, though, because Curtis Granderson came up and singled. Lagares, one of the speedier Mets, was—unlike Castro—able to score from second. The Mets were ahead, 2–1.

The home team added a home run in the sixth, with d'Arnaud literally bruising the Apple (somebody would cheekily apply a large bandage to its top the next day). A Granderson sac fly brought home Lagares in the seventh. Harvey pitched with a 4–1 lead until there were two out in the eighth. Kyle Schwarber, one of those extremely dangerous Chicago sluggers, got to him with a bases-empty homer and Matt exited to an outsize ovation, having filed seven-and-two-thirds innings featuring nine strikeouts and only four hits surrendered. It was hard to recall that there'd been any thought that he might not pitch in the playoffs at all. Familia collected the final four outs and the Mets were 4–2 winners.

Daniel Murphy was just getting started.

* * *

Game Two, played in prime time on Sunday the 18th, was even colder and the Cubs' starter was even more daunting. Jake Arrieta had such a sterling season you'd have thought he pitched for the Dodgers. As it was, he loomed as the only obstacle to Clayton Kershaw or Zack Greinke capturing the Cy Young. Arrieta won 22 games, pitched to a 1.77 ERA and hadn't lost a decision since late July. The Mets saw him for 16 innings in 2015 and scored all of two runs off him.

Though the Mets had made one roster move between the NLDS and the NLCS, swapping out Erik Goeddel for Sean Gilmartin, they hadn't done anything absurd like release Daniel Murphy after Game One. When Game Two started in downright frozen Citi Field, they still retained the services of Murph, and Murph continued to function to form.

Arrieta, not so much. In his very first inning, he gave up a leadoff single to Granderson, an RBI double to David Wright and—stop me if you've heard this before—a home run to Daniel Murphy. This one was a two-run job that staked Noah Syndergaard to a 3–0 lead. In the second, Curtis defended his territory particularly well, pulling in a potential Chris Coghlan home run at the right field wall in what you might call Grandy Chavez-style. The more this postseason went on, the better Granderson performed.

It took me a spell to warm to the ex-Yankee . . . like all of 2014 and most of 2015. He didn't hit much most of his first year and he just seemed too personable to possibly be real. How could someone whose batting average was that low seem so pleasant all the time? He worked the rope line of fan relations like a small-state governor seeking his third term. The man was running unopposed, yet took nothing for granted.

If you were eight years old and your teacher asked you to draw a "really good baseball player," you'd draw Curtis Granderson. Even when he wasn't producing, he always looked the part and he certainly filled the role. When Curtis was eight, I imagine he started making lists of what he'd do when he became that really good baseball player. At the top of the list must've been "always be good to people, even when I'm not playing well." I've never seen anyone embrace that type of self-imposed responsibility more diligently. He greets little kids as pals. He smiles broadly at ladies of an advanced vintage. He signs anything and poses with everyone. He slaps his glove on his head when beginning an interview and leaves it there, all while keeping a straight, professional face. He takes his time and never seems perfunctory. I've seen him, more than once, pause from his on-deck duties to insert himself into front-row selfies upon request. It's so beyond too good to be true it made me cynically wonder what the hell he was up to.

Just helping the Mets win a pennant, apparently.

The Mets would cobble together an extra run in the third and Kris Bryant would double home Dexter Fowler in the sixth, but the game was all but put away on Murph's first fair contact. Thor, amid the kind of Arctic winds you'd intuitively assume a mythic Viking might embrace, lasted five-and-two-thirds innings (Syndergaard's roots are Danish, but he's a born Texan). The Cubs gathered only three hits off him while striking out nine times. Jon Niese, Addison Reed, Tyler Clippard, and Familia kept them scoreless following Noah's exit. The Mets won, 4–1, and carried a two-nothing series lead to Chicago.

Irrespective of curses, that, too, figured to be Murph's kind of town.

BROOM WITH A VIEW

et the record show something didn't go the Mets' way at Wrigley Field. In the top of the sixth in Game Three, with the Mets having just taken a 3–2 lead, Wilmer Flores poked a line drive into right field. It shouldn't have been more than a single, but Jorge Soler dove and completely missed it. The ball rolled directly toward Wrigley's famed ivy. Michael Conforto, who was on first, took off and scored easily. Flores wound up on third with an obvious triple.

Except this was Wrigley and the ivy long ago spawned a ground rule about balls like the one hit by Wilmer getting stuck in there. It did indeed take a Cub bounce and tangle itself where no defender could grab it. Center fielder Dexter Fowler did what other outfielders in other parks did when balls hopped over walls. He threw his hands in the air to signal to the umpires that this ball was inaccessible.

The umpires agreed. Terry Collins argued, but to no avail. Even though common sense said there was no way Conforto wouldn't have scored, he had to be sent back to third and Flores had to be planted at second. It was a ground-rule double.

What a bad break. What an injustice. What a bunch of . . .

Well, actually, it was a bunch of nothing in the end. It was a bunch of nothing in the middle. Conforto was only on first because Miguel Montero couldn't handle strike three in the at-bat prior to Flores's. And the Mets got a run out of that because Yoenis Cespedes was on third. And Cespedes was on third because he'd stolen it from second and was on second because Lucas Duda, of all people, bunted him over from first. The Mets had already manufactured a run in the sixth. They were ahead yet again after not having trailed at all in this game or any game.

So one thing went wrong for them. Boo-freaking-hoo, as somebody drowning his sorrows in the vicinity of Waveland Avenue would be forgiven for thinking. The Cubs were a hot number heading into the NLDS, but they'd gone cold.

* * *

First off, they were totally Murphless.

Secondly, they made the mistake of playing the team that was Murphful.

Thirdly, Daniel Murphy wouldn't stop being Daniel Murphy. His third-inning home run off Kyle Hendricks—his third in the series, his sixth in the postseason—put the Mets up, 2–1. That was after Kyle Schwarber homered off Jacob deGrom in the bottom of the first, which sounds pretty good from a Cub standpoint, except nobody was on and it didn't happen until after Cespedes had driven in David Wright in the top of the first.

True, Soler had tied the game with his own solo homer in the fourth (he wasn't in right for his defense), and true, the ivy couldn't have been more of a home field advantage for them. But though Game Three, on Tuesday, October 20, stayed close, it was tilting inevitably toward the Mets.

Tilt it did. The Cubs were well into their bullpen when the Mets pushed across a couple of insurance runs in the seventh (Murphy was in the middle of that rally, too). DeGrom stayed for seven, allowing only the two solo home runs and two other hits while striking out seven. In a familiar refrain, Tyler Clippard pitched a scoreless eighth and Jeurys Familia a perfect ninth. The Mets were 5–2 winners, ivy notwithstanding.

* * *

This was a best-of-seven series. The Mets were up three games to none. The Red Sox once fell behind by three games in a League Championship Series and prevailed, but they were the only such example. The odds heavily favored the Mets to win their fifth pennant. The only questions were whether they'd sweep and whether Daniel Murphy would continue his home run streak. He had gone deep in every game since since Game Three of the NLDS.

On Wednesday, October 21, in the top of the first, the Mets basically answered the first question. Duda clouted a three-run homer. Travis d'Arnaud came up behind him and homered, too. The Mets were ahead, 4–0. In the top of the second, they reiterated the answer to that first question when Duda doubled home two more runs.

Steven Matz had a 6–0 lead that stayed intact until the fourth when the Cubs scratched out one run. The kid from Long Island seemed in position to earn the decision that would send his team to the World Series, but with two out and two on in the bottom of the fifth, Collins got nervous— no lead is safe at Wrigley Field, etc.—and replaced him with Bartolo Colon. Colon struck out Kris Bryant to end any semblance of a Cub threat. Too bad for Matz the pitcher, but not bad at all for Matz the lifelong Mets fan and current Mets teammate.

With two out in the top of the eighth and Fernando Rodney pitching, Wright walked, bringing up Murphy. This was probably going to be Daniel's last chance to expand on NLCS history.

Here's what he did with it, per Howie Rose:

"Here's the 1-1 to Murph. Swing and a high fly ball, well hit, right-center . . . it's got a chance . . . it's near the wall . . . HE DID IT! ANOTHER HOME RUN FOR MURPHY! He hits it into the first row of the bleachers to the right of the four-hundred foot mark! The Daniel Murphy fairy tale, at least in this series, is pretty well complete. Murphy has now homered in six straight postseason games. A two-run homer, the Mets lead it eight to one, Murphy took a slow trot around the bases, he's prancing into the dugout now, you can NOT BELIEVE what has become of Daniel Murphy!"

* * *

"Go ahead, find something to say, Josh," Howie challenged his partner, Josh Lewin. "I'm out."

So were the descendants of the World Champions of 1908 and the National League champions of 1945, to say nothing of the heretofore imposing Cub club of 2015. According to *Back to the Future II*, the Chicago

Cubs were destined to win the World Series on this very date. Clearly, the movie was not a documentary.

Here in the present, the Cubs' season sweep of the Mets had been inverted and that blue "W" their supporters so enjoyed brandishing had been turned upside down by the visiting fans who clustered in the stands behind the Met dugout. Like the Dodgers, the Cubs had been Murphed into extinction. Bryant chipped Clippard for a two-run shot in the eighth, but it was the epitome of too little, too late.

Collins, as had become his habit, called on Familia to pitch the ninth. Jeurys inherited a five-run lead, but there was something plenty substantial to save, regardless of the 8–3 score. There were two quick outs, a walk, an indifferently defended taking of second and, at last, three balls and two strikes on Fowler.

Howie once more:

"Here's the payoff pitch from Familia to Fowler. On the way . . . and it's IN THERE, STRIKE THREE CALLED!! THE METS WIN THE PENNANT!! THE NEW YORK METS HAVE WON THE NATIONAL LEAGUE PENNANT!! PUT IT IN THE BOOKS!! The New York Mets, for the first time in fifteen years, are champions of the National League!"

* * *

Fifteen long years and four short games. The Mets never trailed in a single inning. They outpitched the Cubs, outfielded the Cubs, outhit the Cubs, and had one more Daniel Murphy than the Cubs. Murph put the "M" in MVP, taking the award with a batting average of .529, an OPS of 1.850 and that indelible string of home runs. Nobody else in the history of major league baseball—nobody—had ever homered in six consecutive postseason games. Between the NLDS and NLCS, he'd posted seven home runs, 11 RBIs and batted .421.

Most importantly, his team was going to the World Series. By extension, so were his team's fans.

At the moment the Mets clinched their 2015 pennant, they didn't know the identity of their next opponent. In the American League, the Royals were leading the Blue Jays three games to two. The ALCS was being played in Canada, which seemed apropos, considering whatever was going on over there was completely foreign to me. My October focus had been devoted solely to the Mets, wherever they were. While watching the visitors at Wrigley launch their latest celebratory frenzy in road grays, Howie briefly considered whether the NL champs might be soon headed to Toronto or Kansas City and determined, "Right now, the New York Mets don't care."

Neither did I. I was still wrapping my mind around what was guaranteed to be run up the Citi Field flagpole.

LONG MAY IT WAVE

The temptation after a night like the one when the Mets finished off their sweep of the Cubs and claimed the fifth pennant in their history is to say this is what makes being a Mets fan worthwhile.

That's nonsense. It's been worthwhile all along.

It was worthwhile the first time you picked up something resembling a ball or a bat and identified with the man on TV, the one who threw the ball faster or swung the bat harder than you ever could.

It was worthwhile when you decided that it might be fun to play baseball, but that *watching* baseball with all your heart and all your soul would be more your forte.

It was worthwhile when you discovered you could wear shirts and caps with the same letters the players on your team wore and you could collect pictures of those players and you could read about them and you could keep watching them on TV and once in a while, if you were lucky, you could go and see them play their games in person.

It was really worthwhile to learn it wasn't just you who enjoyed these things. You were part of a community, a tribe, something bigger than yourself. Those who shared your enthusiasm for this stuff were not necessarily exactly like you, but they were close enough. And you grew close to them.

* * *

In winter, you counted the days until the next baseball season with them. Through spring and summer and into fall, you counted the years until the next *great* baseball season with them. You reassured each other one was coming. Until it did, you enjoyed as best you could the ones you were given.

You relished, because you're a Mets fan, all those years between pennants: the years they came kind of close, the years they came achingly close, the years they came nowhere near close. Sometimes the teams associated with those years darkened your mood, but it never occurred to you your team wasn't part of your life, and you never for a second didn't feel at home with the people who weren't necessarily exactly like you, but they understood what you were going through better than anybody else could. They were going through it, too.

They were your fellow Mets fans. Their commitment was your commitment. You were, by dint of common bond, close to them, and together you dreamed of a night when your team would do something that was becoming unfathomable to the lot of you, like make it to a World Series.

All of that was worthwhile. It was worthwhile whenever you started rooting for the New York Mets. It was worthwhile when the Mets couldn't win a pennant in the 14 seasons that succeeded 2000. It was worthwhile as the Mets went about coalescing into the kind of team that could win a pennant in 2015.

When the Mets did win that flag, after sweeping the Cubs . . . yeah, that was pretty darn worthwhile. Maybe even extraordinarily so.

* * *

Thus, congratulations were in order. However long you had been a Mets fan at the instant October 21, 2015, went in the books as a blue-and-orange-letter day, that night was for you. You may have gone back to April of 1962. Hell, you may have come along in October of 2015. The depth of feeling may have differed, but the feeling was the same.

We won something. We did nothing to win it and we did everything to win it. We're the fans. That's how we roll. It makes perfect sense in our minds, and judging by the reaction of the actual Mets to their fans when they emerged from the visitors' clubhouse at Wrigley to celebrate with a gaggle of them, they don't seem to mind how much we feel a part of what they do.

Even if it seemed Daniel Murphy did it all by himself.

Murph would be the first to credit his teammates. It was his endearing tic in all those postgame press conferences to deflect praise. Indeed, there was plenty of it to go around.

* * *

No, Murph, a Met since 2008, didn't do it alone, no matter how certain you were that he could have had it been necessary. It wasn't. He won the pennant alongside David Wright, from 2004; and Jon Niese, from 2008; and Lucas Duda (generator of five essential Game Four RBIs) from 2010; not to mention a procession of Mets who began to stream into our consciousness in 2012 and 2013 when we were convinced a season like 2015 was still light years away: Nieuwenhuis, Harvey, Familia, Lagares, Flores, d'Arnaud. It wasn't seamless and it didn't always register as logical as 2013 became 2014—*Why Granderson? Why Colon? Who's deGrom?*—but something was happening. Even as we alternated in our derision and dismissiveness (defense mechanisms as much as the products of dispassionate analysis), the Metropolitan plates were shifting.

Onto our hopeful terrain strode Michael Cuddyer, Sean Gilmartin, Kevin Plawecki, Noah Syndergaard, Steven Matz, Michael Conforto, Kelly Johnson, Tyler Clippard, Yoenis Cespedes, Addison Reed, and—because Juan Uribe and Ruben Tejada were hurting—Matt Reynolds. Nearly half the team was new for 2015. They had never lost with the Mets. They joined a cluster of players who had matured and persevered and survived until they could win as Mets. It wasn't an obvious championship roster until you watched them play as one under Terry Collins, perhaps the most underestimated manager in modern major league history.

* * *

Once they all came together and showed what they could do, there was no doubt. Same as there were no losses to the Cubs. Same as there was no feeling like that we felt when Jeurys Familia struck out Dexter Fowler looking on October 21, 2015—with the respective exceptions of Nolan Ryan, Tug McGraw, Jesse Orosco, and Mike Hampton retiring Tony Gonzalez,

Dan Driessen, Kevin Bass, and Rick Wilkins under similar circumstances in 1969, 1973, 1986, and 2000.

Those were the first four seasons in which the New York Mets ever won the National League pennant. As of 2015, there was a fifth. We'd have to mentally revise the total that had been ingrained in us for a generation. We'd been so used to saying the Mets have been to the World Series four times. Now we'd have to say five. I was sure we could make the adjustment. The Mets adjusted from perennial losers to dynamic winners in 2015. We Mets fans adjusted from thinking this fifth pennant might never get here to embracing it as it arrived: built by Alderson; shaped by Collins; earned by pitching; secured by Murphness; sprayed by champagne; baptized by tears.

We never had to change our ways, though. We may not have always believed, but we were always capable of Believing. It was in us the whole time. Our capability just had to be tapped.

HOW WE GOT (ONLY) SO FAR

NO OTHER

The Mets were in the World Series. Not the "postseason" any longer, not the "next round," certainly not the MLB Finals. The 2015 Mets insinuated themselves into an institution that captured America's imagination for the bulk of the 20th century and still held a certain sway over everyday conversation when it came around annually in the 21st.

The World Series may have been surpassed by the Super Bowl for primacy among the professional sports championships, and its television viewership may have diminished in this age of so many other things to look at, but it was still the World Series. Even people who barely knew baseball existed were conscious of the one event that decided its championship, especially when it was taking place where they lived.

My favorite part of the World Series was the part before it started, the part where my fellow New Yorkers who *never* talked baseball with me couldn't stop talking baseball with me. These weren't Mets fans. They were just people who had noticed I was a Mets fan. They wanted a piece of the trending topic. Instead of having my routine mania ignored or vaguely pitied as it usually was, I became—probably via the sight of my beaten and battered seventeen-year-old Starter jacket (which had replaced the previous beaten and battered seventeen-year-old Starter jacket in my wardrobe seventeen years before)—their October touchstone, their link to legitimacy and their way into what all the fuss was about.

At least until the next Mets fan came walking by.

Before and after it became known that the Mets would be going up against the Royals, I was subject to essentially the same set of questions and comments, repeated in a loop.

"You think they can win?"
"You must be excited!"
"Are you going to any of the games?"
"This is really great!"

My response to all of it was "yes," which reflected my general giddiness in the interregnum that filled the days between the playoffs and the Fall Classic. The Mets pervaded every facet of existence in these parts. Old jackets came out of closets. New caps flew out of Modell's. Store windows were decorated as if for blue and orange Christmas. Team flags fronted porches and yards. Special preview sections wrapped the tabloids. Daniel Murphy faced out from the cover of *Sports Illustrated*. Tribute videos plastered YouTube. Mr. Met, elevated to goodwill ambassador for an entire region, conducted the Metropolitan Opera orchestra in a classy rendition of "Meet the Mets" on the plaza at Lincoln Center. Radio stations played delectably cringeworthy song parodies ("God bless Daniel Murphy" is one jury-rigged lyric that will forever stay with me whenever I hear "It's Raining Men," thanks to WCBS-FM's musical handiwork). When the Mets were through working out and made any kind of public appearance—at Barclays Center to watch the recently resettled Islanders; on the set of the visiting *Jimmy Kimmel Live*—they were immersed in standing ovations. The local news led with Mets, Mets, and more Mets. County governments on both sides of the city line sponsored pep rallies.

Pep was not an element I had difficulty rallying. I hazily remembered New York being like this in 1969 and 1973. I totally remembered New York being like this in 1986.

Funny, I didn't quite remember New York being like this in 2000.

* * *

The World Series fever that should have gripped the city on behalf of the Mets fifteen years earlier was preempted by hype for the Subway Series.

We had to share that particular stage with New York's American League entry, which is to say we were lucky to rate co-star billing.

The Yankee dynasty of the Joe Torre era was a tough act to interrupt. The Bobby Valentine Mets surely had their moments circa 1999 and 2000, but they were destined to play out in the background, even during the 2000 World Series. Winning that Subway Series would have been grand, but it wouldn't have changed what its prelude was like. The Mets were treated like the "other team" in their hometown. We might as well have flown in from Cincinnati. It had begun being like that in New York around 1993, amid the Yankees' auspicious ascendance and the Mets' dreadful decline, and it didn't really stop until Jeurys Familia struck out Dexter Fowler.

Now, in the sweet, embraceable autumn of 2015, there was no longer any otherness to being a Mets fan in New York. I tried to be mature and not worry about the municipal competition all these years, but I realized that when it comes to late October, this town ain't big enough for the two of us. We had to, as the spiffy 7 Line T-shirt commanded, TAKE BACK NEW YORK.

We did. Or the Mets did. They won more and longer than their counterparts. They won so much and so long that they were going to the World Series. Their usually noisy neighbors completely receded from the scene. If you wanted a baseball team in New York . . . if you wanted in on the action that was defining life as we were living it . . . the Mets were your only ticket.

I guess you could call it a bandwagon. I called it about frigging time.

A ROYAL PAIN

L et us dispense with the conceit of building suspense and simply reiterate a result that is widely known and universally lamented among the likely readers of this volume. The New York Mets lost the World Series in five games to the Kansas City Royals. The Mets led in all five games. In four of them, the Mets held a lead entering the eighth or ninth inning; they won only one of them.

There's no escaping the paper bag the Mets couldn't hit, pitch or field their way out of when it mattered most. The Royals might as well have done business as the Mike Moustakas Traveling All-Stars & Motor Kings. Once they barnstormed their way through the Mets, they presumably brought their act to an adoring public up and down the Midwestern countryside.

Artificial turf is no longer in vogue, but the Royals played Whiteyball like it used to be. They stole bases at will (something the Mets had done so well against the Cubs), they took advantage of physical and mental lapses, they converted opportunities into runs and they gave the Mets few inches with which to work. Unassuming Ned Yost channeled his K. C. predecessor Whitey Herzog. Terry Collins, with only so many buttons to push, was no match, nor were his players.

The Mets' five-game loss was a team effort. Daniel Murphy's tenure as emperor of the baseball universe did not extend beyond the National League playoffs. Yoenis Cespedes couldn't have been less valuable. Jeurys Familia's infallibility expired. The rest of the bullpen seemed awfully thin. David Wright made a bad throw and a dubious decision. Lucas Duda made a horrible throw on the heels of that dubious decision by the Captain and another by the manager. Travis d'Arnaud shouldn't have bothered throwing at all. The vaunted starting pitching generally lived up to its burgeoning reputation, but the opposing rotation did enough vaunting of its own to neutralize the advantage.

And yet, the Mets were hardly ever out of any game. Except for maybe Game Two, they were as in as could be in every contest, but as the Washington Nationals could have told them in September, there's a difference between leading and winning. The Mets led. The Royals won.

Ouch.

* * *

Game One at Kauffman Stadium on Tuesday, October 27 was one pitch into the bottom of the first inning when the Mets fell one run behind. Matt Harvey's first pitch to Alcides Escobar became an inside-the-park home run. Cespedes nearly caught it, but instead kicked it. It was that kind of Series from the get-go.

The Mets strung together single runs in the fourth, fifth, and sixth against Edinson Volquez— including the first of Curtis Granderson's three Series homers—but Harvey gave back the 3–1 lead in a blink and the teams were tied after six. The spirit of Bill Buckner inhabited Eric Hosmer just long enough to put the Mets ahead in the eighth. With two out and Juan Lagares on second, Wilmer Flores grounded a ball around the Royal first baseman's legs. It was akin to our best play in the 1986 World Series and no Mets fan minded seeing it reincarnated now.

Familia was charged with protecting the 4–3 lead in the ninth. He got the first out just fine. He got second and third outs, too, but not before Alex Gordon lined one of his quick-pitch sinkers over the center field fence. Quick as could be, the game was tied at four.

* * *

It was the last thing that went quickly all night. The Mets, whose previous engagement in Missouri, at Busch Stadium in July, didn't end for 18 innings, were reluctant entrants in another marathon. It would be their longest World Series game ever, both in terms of innings (14) and time (5:09). It would also be among their most frustrating.

The clock struck *It's Still On?* The Mets were going to need to be perfect, but it was apparently too late to expect them to be anything more than Mets. One of their former members, the tall and soft-tossing starter Chris Young, pitched against them from the 12th through the 14th, and kept them off the board. Current relievers Addison Reed, Jon Niese, and Bartolo Colon gave what they could, but the relief corps was bound to give out if Mets hitters couldn't take what was there for the snatching.

So they gave. Colon, in his third inning of doing what he doesn't normally do, was undone from jump in the bottom of the 14th as valiant Captain Wright first misplayed and then flung indiscriminately a hot leadoff grounder from Escobar. Escobar was safe and doom hung heavy in the night air. Ben Zobrist, who the Mets really should have picked up at the trading deadline just to avoid confronting him repeatedly and futilely in their first World Series game in fifteen years, singled Escobar to third. Runners on the corners, nobody out . . . this would have been the ideal moment to have Fox's picture and sound disappear as it had earlier in the game.

Anytime you can't hear Joe Buck is ideal, actually.

Collins went to his intentional walk tactics, moves that twice allowed Colon to wriggle out of the 12th (and if Bartolo can wriggle, there's hope for us all). When your only reasonable answer to first and third is to make it first, second, and third, you're not playing to your strong suit. The Mets had their strongest suit, Familia, fold for the first time in three months in the ninth. Maybe it just wasn't going to be their night.

And it wasn't. After walking Lorenzo Cain to load the bases, Hosmer lofted a deep fly to Granderson, who threw as strongly as he was capable of throwing, but his effort wasn't strong enough to nab Escobar at the plate.

The Royals prevailed, 5–4. They got to bounce around like silly schoolkids who'd inhaled one too many Pixy Stix past their bedtime. Once they pulled themselves apart from their glorious embrace, they were invited to relax and pull up a chair on all the postgame gabfests. The Mets, who lost their fifth World Series Game One (but the only one that counted at the moment), were assigned the unenviable role of other team. Their interrogations would have to be grimly conducted among tight spaces and sullen faces. "Just one game," they probably said. It was too late to pay a whole lot of attention.

Salvation lies within knowing second games of seven-game series can turn your fortunes around. But there was no salvation on Wednesday night the 28th. There was instead Salvador Perez putting down his fingers and Johnny Cueto doing the rest. Cueto, whom the Mets outlasted at Citi Field in late June, wasn't budging at the K. He stayed in for all nine innings and gave up only two hits to the Mets. Jacob deGrom would have had to have been exceptionally sharp to keep up. He wasn't. The Mets lost the first World Series complete game in a half-dozen years, 7–1. This one was done in under three hours. The Royals could win slow. The Royals could win fast. The Mets, all of a sudden, could not win at all.

Their last reasonable chance to change the momentum of the World Series would be Game Three, Friday night, October 30, at home. New York was willing to overlook the hole they had dug for themselves and invited them to start fresh.

* * *

Game Three was my first in-person World Series game ever. It was like going to a regular baseball game but more so. You'd see people outside the ballpark for a regular baseball game. You saw *everybody* outside Citi Field before Game Three. Every media outlet that had the right deal with MLB had a set built. Every media outlet that didn't have one had a reporter doing a live stand-up. I decided on the spur of the moment to be one of those dopes who waves his Mets cap at the first TV camera he sees (quite the bucket list I've got there).

Placards were being distributed on the steps down from the 7 train. Merchandise was being sold once you descended the steps. High-fives were being exchanged all along your route to your gate of choice. This wasn't normal Citi Field behavior. But this wasn't a normal circumstance.

This was the World Series. This was what we'd rooted for. This was as big as I imagined it. The American flag was gargantuan. The national anthem was performed by Billy Joel. The ceremonial first pitch was thrown by Mike Piazza. The space between innings was larger than most Manhattan studio apartments.

Into this heightened atmosphere stepped 6' 6" Noah Syndergaard. His first pitch was ceremonial as well, designed to announce the Mets' presence with authority and concomitantly place Escobar on his rear end. It worked, and that, too, was big. All we'd heard for two games was how the Royals aggressively "attack" and "ambush." Escobar was a notorious first-ball swinger. On this night, he'd have to sit on the ground against his will.

We let out a cheer equal to the size of the statement.

I'd love to tell you Thor set the tone from that first pitch forward, but the Royals dusted themselves off and scored a run right away. Wright answered back with a two-run homer off Yordano Ventura in the bottom of the first—it took him only a dozen seasons to have one of those in a World Series—but the Royals responded just fine, with two more in the second.

Then the Mets we'd all come to see came to life. Syndergaard, in the best tradition of National League pitchers hitting in National League parks, singled to open the third. Granderson homered to give the Mets a 4–3 lead. Michael Conforto broke out of a long slump to drive in another run in the fourth. And in the sixth, Juan Uribe—pronounced fit and able to join the fun (at the expense of Matt Reynolds's pristine roster spot)—pinch-singled and keyed the four-run rally that put the game away. Thor went six for the win and got credit for the lines of the night in the postgame chat sessions. The Royals were complaining about that first pitch, the one that literally floored Escobar. Syndergaard wasn't apologizing.

- "My intent on that pitch was to make them feel uncomfortable, and I feel like I did just that."
- "If they have a problem with me throwing inside, then they can meet me sixty feet, six inches away."
- "I feel like it really made a statement to start the game off—that you guys can't dig in and get too aggressive because I'll come in there."

The Royals came into Citi Field and lost. They didn't like the feeling. They didn't have to get accustomed to it.

Game Four, on Saturday night the 31st, looked pretty good for quite a while. Tim McGraw threw out the first pitch, so of course we had to Believe. Steven Matz tugged at our hopestrings by making his first three innings scoreless. Denton True "Chris" Young gave up a leadoff homer to Conforto in the bottom of the third and another run besides. Matz nursed the 2–0 lead into the fifth. Kansas City nicked him for a run, but Conforto got it back in the bottom of the inning with his second leadoff home run of the night, this one off Danny Duffy. Michael became the only Met not named Gary Carter to hit two home runs in one World Series game.

With the opportunity to match the hero status of sandwich back at the Se-Port Deli in East Setauket, Matz found himself being bitten into by the ravenous Royals. Zobrist doubled, Cain singled, and the Mets' lead was down to 2–1. Collins started managing, replacing Matz with Niese and then Niese with Colon to get out of the sixth. It took three pitchers, but the Mets still led by a run.

Each of the next three relievers to enter the game—Luke Hochevar and Ryan Madson for the Royals, Reed for the Mets—pitched a scoreless half-inning. Tyler Clippard, who was acquired in July in the interest of bullpen stability, was next. He retired his first batter in the top of the eighth, but walked the two who followed, Zobrist and Cain. Collins removed him in favor of Familia who, like Clippard, was used for an inning with a six-run lead the night before. Terry wanted a five-out save.

He'd get no such thing.

* * *

Familia grounded Hosmer to second. Murphy, who'd worked long and hard to resemble a major league second baseman, was unmasked as something less on Halloween night. He fumbled the ground ball. Zobrist raced home, Cain went to third and Hosmer was on first. The game was tied.

And the Series was lost. From where I sat in Promenade, I swore I could feel it leaving Citi Field, perhaps to get a jump on traffic, maybe so it wouldn't have to watch what was about to unfold.

Technically, the World Series continued, purely to the Mets' detriment. Moustakas placed a grounder outside the reach of Murphy, a base hit that scored Cain and sent Hosmer to third. The Royals were ahead, 4–3. Perez followed with another single, scoring Hosmer. It was 5–3.

The Mets went down in order in the eighth against Wade Davis. They hadn't had a hit since the fifth. Hansel Robles threw a perfect ninth, but any hay that might have been made was sabotaged in the bottom of the inning. There was a whiff of hope. With one out, Murphy singled. Cespedes singled. Duda, he of the 27 home runs during the regular season and the five RBIs in the pennant-clincher, stood in against Davis. Power versus power, with visions of walk-off drama dancing in what was left of 44,815 heads.

Lucas lined softly to Moustakas at third for the second out. Cespedes loitered between first and second for reasons best known to him. Moustakas fired to first for the third out.

A team effort all around. The Mets were one game from elimination. The fantasy that they could replicate the pattern of nearly three decades before (they'd lost Games One and Two and won Game Three by the same margins in 2015 that they had in 1986) was detonated. It wasn't impossible to imagine they could win three in a row from the Royals, but it did take some wishful thinking to believe it.

* * *

Game Five was Sunday night, November 1, the first game the Mets would ever play in the eleventh month. Maybe the calendar would change our luck. Or maybe the Mets' starting pitcher would transcend luck. For eight innings, luck seemed immaterial.

Harvey had his fastball. Everything else paled by comparison.

Granderson evoked Tommie Agee, Wayne Garrett, and Lenny Dykstra by leading off the game (albeit not a Game Three) with a home run. He'd score the Mets' second run in the sixth after walking and eventually coming around on a single, an error, and a sac fly. Those were the only two runs the Mets scored off Volquez, but with Harvey being Harvey, it didn't seem the Mets would need any more.

The Dark Knight was at his most brilliant when the Mets needed him most. Through eight innings, Matt gave up four hits, one walk and no runs. The Royals, renowned for making contact, struck out nine times. Watching on TV, I wondered how Winnebago had managed such a loud product placement. All I heard was what sounded like "RV! RV!"

Hardly anybody wanted Harvey to leave after eight innings. He'd taken down his last six batters on 15 pitches. The chants were deafening. The stakes were enormous. The pressure was immense.

The manager relented. His instinct was to go to Familia. His decision was to go to Familia. In the dugout, with Fox's cameras rolling, Harvey changed Terry's mind. Matt jogged briskly to the mound to start the ninth, as well as the Mets' ultimate downfall.

* * *

Harvey lost his leadoff batter, Cain, on a full count, issuing his second walk of the game. This might have been the ideal juncture to bring in Familia. Collins waited.

On the first pitch, Cain stole second (the Royals would steal four bases in the game and seven in the Series, never once getting caught). On the second pitch, Hosmer connected for a double into the left field corner. Cain scored easily. The Royals' deficit was one run.

Now Harvey was coming out and Familia was coming in, two or one batters too late. Some of this is hindsight. We know Harvey didn't get the first batter out. We know a run happened almost immediately thereafter. We also know that those eight innings in which Harvey blanked Kansas City didn't happen on some other night. We know the season rode on Harvey's right arm and it rode almost to a sixth game.

Almost. But not quite.

Familia faced his third save situation of the Series, though he had yet to register a save. All it would take was three outs and the stranding of Hosmer to make it happen. This fifth game could still be won, this World Series could still go on.

Instead, Moustakas moved Hosmer to third with a grounder to Duda. One out, one very much on. Perez came up. Hosmer took a daring lead off third. Perez grounded toward short. Wright anxiously cut in front of Flores to grab the ball. Hosmer, with no defender at third, waited out Wright's perfunctory glance back to the bag. Wright threw to first. Hosmer took off for home. Duda made the out at first, then turned and fired to d'Arnaud.

A good throw probably would have nailed the runner. Duda's throw sailed somewhere into Corona. Hosmer was safe, the game was tied, and that was pretty much that.

The game would unfurl for a while longer. Jeurys, saddled with a third blown save, got out of the ninth. The Mets went to bat and did nothing against Kelvin Herrera, guaranteeing extras. Familia was perfect in the top of the tenth, his teammates futile in its bottom. Niese worked around a single and a steal in the eleventh. Hochevar threw two shutout innings. Reed came on to pitch the 12th, which is when the whole sordid affair was mercifully put out of its misery. The Royals recorded four hits, stole a base, and scored five runs. The foregone conclusion became reality at 12:34 a.m. on Monday, November 2 as Wilmer Flores took called strike three from Wade Davis. The Mets lost Game Five, 7–2, and the 2015 World Series, four games to one.

* * *

If you didn't like the outcome, perhaps you'd accept as a consolation prize a touch of perspective. The 2014 Mets were mathematically eliminated from postseason contention in their 154th game. In 2013, the game that reduced the Mets' playoff chances to absolute zero was their 144th. From 2009 to 2012, the so-called tragic numbers were, respectively, 144, 151, 149, and 147. For six years, the Mets played a handful of games beyond their elimination and then they went home.

In 2015, the Mets lasted 176 games, which arithmetic reminds us is a lot more and logic assures is a lot better. We kept playing into October. We kept playing into November. It was what we wanted—just not all we wanted. The 176th game and the finality it brought to bear assaulted our Met emotions at the moment of impact like Chase Utley slamming into Ruben Tejada. You don't easily shake off that kind of an ending.

But you never forget the journey that took you so far.

UNPRECEDENTED

From the moment 2015 came into view, Mets fans with any kind of memory instinctively searched for a precedent in their franchise's history to explain in advance what would happen next. Was this going to be another 1968 or 1983, years talent began to gather in earnest even if the standings didn't yet reflect the progress? Could we, with so much good young pitching, get a 1984 up in here? We'd gladly take surpassing .500 and making a spirited playoff run as a sign that a corner had finally and definitively been turned. As the impact of a spectacular start sunk in, maybe what we had on our hands was the reincarnation of 1969! When the injuries took a toll after that spectacular start, was it 1972 all over again?

When Terry Collins was forced to deploy offensively paltry lineups every night, it might as well have been 1962. Dare we dream the Mets make a transformative trade in-season, à la Mike Piazza in 1998? Yoenis Cespedes came aboard and played like a supercharged Donn Clendenon, so between that and the overthrowing of the favored Nationals, 1969 seemed to be the answer. Or was this more a You Gotta Believe 1973 vibe? But the way we dominated in August—that was very 1986ish. Yet when we'd lose a game or two in September, it rained 2007 anxieties.

The Mets posted their first winning record since 2008, first postseason appearance since 2006, and first league title since 2000. Shades of playoff teams from 1999 and 1988 beckoned if you chose to spot them. A baseball season issues you a visa to visit the past as much as you desire. The past is everywhere you want it to be.

But, really, when I look at the 2015 New York Mets, I am borne back ceaselessly into the present, or at least what the present was from the time the Mets gathered their forces for their 54th spring training through the conclusion of their fifth World Series.

* * *

The 2015 Mets gave us an unprecedented campaign. As much as we find familiarity in what we think we recognize from our prior experience, every season is a wholly different creature from those which preceded it. So though there are comparisons to be made and links to be forged, the 2015 Mets were really something we never saw before.

And who's to say when we'll see anything like them again?

Cespedes's surge. Murphy's marvelousness. Granderson's grandeur. Wright's return. Wilmer welling up. The Matt Harvey Show in all its complexity. Rookies Thor, Conforto, and Matz, each maturing in our midst. DeGrom and his hair, each growing in their second year. Familia slamming all those doors. D'Arnaud and Plawecki framing all those strikes. Nieuwenhuis coming out of nowhere. Uribe and Johnson coming to the rescue. Torres racing to the bag. Colon flipping to it from behind his back. Cuddyer and Lagares gracefully stepping aside when asked. Niese and Duda and—as much as he could—Parnell hanging in there after so many seasons. Tejada walking tall after absorbing the worst an unsavory opponent had to unleash. Citi Field clearing its throat and emitting a roar. "The World Series" entering our vocabulary and keeping New York actively talking about whether the Mets would win tonight later in a year than ever before.

* * *

The Mets were still on the clock the night Daylight Savings Time ran its course and Eastern Standard Time was reinstated. The first Sunday in November coincided with Game Five of the World Series. The Mets couldn't turn back the clock as much as we would have liked on November 1. We would have preferred "first world championship since 1986" added to their and our portfolio, but the Royals, who'd waited themselves since 1985, prevented the outcome we craved.

So that clock kept ticking, springing ahead to thirty years and counting as of 2016. What would transpire in the hastily arriving "next year" nobody still soaking in the high of a National League championship could know. But I would guess that for the rest of time, whenever somebody mentions 2015, a Mets fan will smile. And why not? That was the year we won the pennant.

My gosh, that was fun.

ACKNOWLEDGMENTS

Jonathan Larson, composer of "Seasons of Love," asked how does one measure, measure a year? When you're a baseball fan it's simple enough to go to Baseball-Reference, click on the appropriate page and get all you need to know, whether the object of your curiosity is David Wright, Matt Harvey, Jack Leathersich (17 appearances in 2015, 15 of them in Met losses) or Akeel Morris (one game, eight batters faced, only two of them retired). No storehouse of statistics is more vital in the Internet age. In parochial terms, Ultimate Mets Database is no less critical a tool to Mets fans/authors.

Yet there are elements to a baseball season you love that can't be measured by metrics, traditional or advanced. To me, a season like 2015 is defined as much by who I got to share it with as it was by who racked up the hits, run, errors, strikes, balls, and 1-3-1 putouts. I'm blessed with quite a roster in that regard. It includes, but is not limited to the following folks.

Jason Fry, my monstrously talented blogging partner of eleven seasons. Joe Figliola, who I relish meeting up with in the head car on the Babylon line every time the Mets hand out a bobblehead. Sharon Chapman, my companion for the first home game of every postseason series and many games in many less successful seasons. Kevin Chapman, the king of the parking lot where Shea once stood. The Spectors—Garry, Susan, Melanie—who know how to do a lot of things, especially throw a graduation party.

Ryder and Rob Chasin, who have brightened at least one evening for my wife and me every August since 2010. Ben Rosenfield, budding lawyer and gracious soul. Brian Sokoloff, practicing attorney and dedicated fan. Daniel Gold, the self-appointed Spirit of '69 on Halloween night at Citi Field. Rob Emproto, who gives championship hugs whenever a pennant is won. Mark Simon, who makes statistics come more alive than any writer I know. Matt Silverman, whose look back on the 2015 Mets sometime before 2040 will fit right in with his wonderful work on the 1969, 1973, and 1986 clubs.

Larry Jabbonsky, who helped make much possible. Andrea Foote, who threw in the towel and then another towel. Larry Arnold, partly for surprise entry to NLDS Game Four, mostly for converting Justin Arnold to the cause. Sam Maxwell, who converted to Metsdom so fully you'd think he was born this way. Ed Witty, who was born this way but didn't know it until he was about to turn fifty. Jeff Reiter, the Cubs fan who couldn't have been happier for his friend the Mets fan. Frank Lennox, the Cubs fan who adopted the Nationals when the Expos moved to Washington and was thus compelled to congratulate me twice.

Jay Goldberg, who provides baseball fans of all stripe a beautiful home away from home at the Bergino Clubhouse. Gary Mintz and Bill Kent, keepers of the flame for the New York Giants, the team I would have rooted for had I come along sooner. Mark Weinstein, who keeps asking to hear more about that. Jerry Evans, who brought some Left Coast cool with him in April. Andrew Richter, the photographer a once-in-a-lifetime deconstruction deserved. Mark Mehler, whose Met pronoun of choice is second-person singular, though I'm pretty sure that for all his "you," he's deep down one of us. Charlie Hangley, preternaturally warm no matter how chilly the night game might be. David Roth, who made Closing Day complete when stopped by to say hi. Emily Bernstein, without whose presence a Met postseason is incomplete.

Michael Garry, Jon Springer, and Jim Haines, who were as taken by the August noise on the Citi Field stairwells as I was. Paul (a.k.a. batmagadanleadoff) whose last name continues to escape me but whose company never doesn't delight me. Richie Giustiniani, whose last name I hope I've gotten right after seventeen years. Kevin Connell, perhaps the last Mets fan who still properly loathes the Braves for 1999. Jodie Remick, who penciled me in for Opening Day 2016 while my mind was still lost in thoughts of 2015. The guys from the *Tide*, who've been my pals since I wore the first edition of the Magic is Back T-shirt. Mr. Stem, who scours tag sales on my behalf and delivers me otherwise unimagined Met treasures.

The entire *Faith and Fear in Flushing* community represents the best readers and commenters in all of baseball blogging. Mets bloggers and even the murky-reputationed "Mets Twitter" are some of the greatest people with whom I've had the pleasure of interacting. And in a galling yet unintended act of short shrift, anybody I've failed to mention by name above or below . . . thank you, too.

Adam Rubin's coverage of the Mets is the orange and blue standard. When I wasn't sure of a particular detail anywhere between the first callisthenic of February to the final pitch of November, I knew his ESPN.com archive was the place to search. Ben Lindbergh wrote a piece for the sadly defunct *Grantland* in 2014 outlining "transaction trees," which led me to realize the roots of the 2015 National League champs stretched all the way back to 1967. Gary Cohen, Howie Rose, and Josh Lewin are all gentlemen, and the opportunity to listen to their calls anew was a fringe benefit of writing this book.

That Ken Samelson of Skyhorse asked me to write this book is proof that it was a good idea, no matter how I executed the task. Thank you as well to publishing pros Jason Katzman, Niels Aaboe, and Julie Ganz for their role in the process of making a book idea a reality.

David "Skid" Rowe is probably his own book. Long story short, he's a Mets fan who grew up in Northern California idolizing Willie Mays and switching his allegiances to a team 3,000 miles from where he lived once the Say Hey Kid returned to New York in 1972. It was Skid's dream to someday move to Queens himself and spend an entire season going to every Mets home game. In 2015, that's exactly what he did. We watched several of those games together and became close friends because of our baseball team. If the Mets produce a highlight film, they'd be most accurate to title it The Year of Skid.

Jeff Hysen is my baseball confidant and somebody who looks out for my best interests more than I do. Jeff wanted this book written before I did. I thank him for listening closely, speaking frankly, and showing me how to use my new phone.

Carlos Briceno is my best friend of more than thirty years, and just when I think he can't surprise me, he blows my mind. He insists on calling himself a bandwagon fan. I will always save him a place on this one.

On the morning of May 20, my wife and I were looking forward to attending that night's Mets game against the Cardinals. The aforementioned Chapmans generously invited us to join them on the Party City Deck to help celebrate their wedding anniversary. We never made it. That same morning, I received a phone call advising me my father had taken ill. The diagnosis was a brain tumor, for which surgery was recommended a couple of days hence. Through my father's lengthy recovery period and eventual contracting of pneumonia, I'd spend far more time in hospitals, rehab and treatment centers. and care facilities than I would at the ballpark (though I eventually seemed to find my way to Citi Field all right). There was nothing good about any of this, but I will always remember how my 2015 season culminated, sitting next to my dad—never much of a baseball fan but caught up in the Mets like the rest of New York—and watching the World Series with him. Even though the last game we watched together was a loss, I'll always treasure those final innings. And while he and I chatted about baseball and other things, I found myself texting pitch to pitch with my sister, who had herself come down with an unusually acute case of Mets fever. My earliest World Series memory was the three of us in the car listening to Game One in 1969. Bringing the Fall Classic full circle with them meant the world to me at the end of 2015.

Stephanie Prince married the biggest Mets fan she ever met and I will forever be grateful. I'm the biggest Stephanie Prince fan you'll ever meet.